GOD'S Little Lessons on Life

For
Graduates

*God Bless you +
Keep you, Nadine*

*Love
X O X O*

HONOR
B O O K S

Honor Books
Tulsa, Oklahoma

Awful Attitude

Cheryl continually complained that she didn't make enough money, couldn't afford the things she wanted, and therefore, wasn't ever going to amount to anything. A counselor said to her, "You're throwing your energy away complaining instead of using it to get ahead."

"But you don't understand. The job is the problem, not me," Cheryl countered.

The counselor said, "Your low-paying job may be a problem and your boss may demand too much, but if you are continually that upset, you are causing *yourself* more harm than either the job or the boss."

"What can I do?" she asked.

The counselor said, "You can't control your boss or the job, but you can control how you *feel* about them. Change your attitude."

Cheryl took her advice. When she stopped whining about her life, people around her noticed. She got a promotion, and with her new job status, she was more marketable. Within several months, she was transferred out of the department into a position with even higher pay and a more supportive boss.

Awful is a state of *attitude*. A change in attitude will change the state of things!

Comfort

Trust in him at all times, O people; pour out your hearts to him, for God is our refuge.

Psalm 62:8

You have turned for me my mourning into dancing; you have put off my sackcloth and clothed me with gladness.

Psalm 30:11 NKJV

[Jesus said] "Therefore you too now have sorrow; but I will see you again, and your heart will rejoice, and no one takes your joy away from you."

John 16:22 NAS

When times are good, be happy; but when times are bad, consider: God has made the one as well as the other.

Ecclesiastes 7:14

Introduction

New beginnings. While a graduation always signifies the end of something, it also means the beginning of a new adventure in life. A new phase. A new opportunity for growth and development. It is crucial to begin that new era with the essential tools for success—good advice, good friends, and good books.

God's Little Lessons on Life for Graduates is the perfect addition to any graduate's collection. It runs the gamut of life's issues, ranging from dealing with life's emotions like anger or loneliness to daily needs such as comfort and wisdom.

The easy-to-read format of *God's Little Lessons on Life for Graduates* lends itself to many uses. It is arranged topically so that it can be used to find answers as situations and circumstances occur, giving solutions for your own life, as well as wisdom to share with others. However, it can also be used as a daily devotional, to build character and strength day by day.

Let *God's Little Lessons on Life for Graduates* keep you on the path to new horizons, prepare you for new challenges, and inspire you to new levels of growth and fulfillment. Don't hesitate—start learning the lessons today!

Table of Contents

Anger

An angry man stirs up strife, and a hot-tempered man abounds in transgression.

Proverbs 29:22 NAS

A gentle answer turns away wrath, but a harsh word stirs up anger.

Proverbs 15:1

The wrath of man does not produce the righteousness of God.

James 1:20 NKJV

Do not associate with one easily angered, or you may learn his ways and get yourself ensnared.

Proverbs 22:24-25

Diffuse Your Anger

The great maestro Toscanini was as well known for his ferocious temper as he was for his outstanding musicianship. During rehearsals, when members of his orchestra played badly, Toscanini often picked up whatever was within reach and hurled it to the floor in disgust. During one rehearsal someone misplayed a note. Its tone reverberated throughout the rehearsal hall. Toscanini frowned and grabbed his quite valuable watch from the director's stand, smashing it to the floor. The watch was broken beyond repair.

Shortly afterward, Toscanini's devoted musicians gave him a gift in a luxurious velvet-lined box. Inside the box were two watches. One of the timepieces was a beautiful gold watch of the best quality and workmanship. The other was a cheap dimestore watch. On the back of the inexpensive watch was an inscription that read: For rehearsals only.

While Toscanini's temper affected replaceable material things, anger quite often destroys irreplaceable things too. An angry word can tear friends or family members apart for years. A quick temper can instill fear in others and bring about bitterness and separation. Anger rarely has a positive outcome, in your own life or in the lives of those around you. Learn how to diffuse it!

Anger

You yourselves are to put off all these: anger,
wrath, malice, blasphemy, filthy language out of
your mouth.

Colossians 3:8 NKJV

He that is slow to anger is better than the mighty;
and he that ruleth his spirit than he that taketh a
city.

Proverbs 16:32 KJV

If you stay calm, you are wise, but if you have a
hot temper, you only show how stupid you are.
Proverbs 14:29 TEV

Cease from anger, and forsake wrath; do not fret,
it leads only to evildoing.
Psalm 37:8 NAS

Choose to Live Above Anger

Victor Frankl was a Jewish psychiatrist who was imprisoned in the Nazi death camps in Germany. His family members were all imprisoned in the same camps and eventually sent to the gas chamber. Frankl never knew if his path would lead to the ovens or if he would be among the "saved" who were forced to shovel the ashes of the dead.

One day, alone and naked in a small room, Frankl realized that he still possessed one last human freedom—Victor Frankl could choose. He could decide within himself how the unthinkable torture and innumerable indignities were going to affect him. He could grow angry and detached, hard and cold like his oppressors. Or he could control his inner environment and find meaning in his suffering and dignity in his existence. Relying heavily on his memory and imagination and using a series of mental, emotional, and moral disciplines, Frankl exercised his freedom of choice and became an inspiration to the prisoners around him.

Though others may control your external circumstances, only you—with God's help—can control how you respond. Choose love, dignity, and control, and you too can live above your anger.

Attitude

As he thinks in his heart, so is he.

Proverbs 23:7 NKJV

A merry heart doeth good like a medicine: but a broken spirit drieth the bones.

Proverbs 17:22 KJV

Happy are those who fear the LORD. Yes, happy are those who delight in doing what he commands.

Psalm 112:1 NLT

When people are happy, they smile, but when they are sad, they look depressed.

Proverbs 15:13 TEV

Lighten Up

The great preacher Charles H. Spurgeon once emphasized to a preaching class that a speaker's facial expressions should harmonize with his sermon. He suggested that "when you speak of Heaven, let your face light up, let it be irradiated with a heavenly gleam, let your eyes shine with reflected glory. But when you speak of Hell, well, then your ordinary face will do."

While we may think it fake to "force" an attitude of cheerfulness or a facial expression, such as a smile, scientific documentation has proved that sustaining a cheerful expression actually uses less muscle power than maintaining a frown. Researchers note that an optimistic, upbeat attitude can more easily defuse pressure and stress than an attitude of pessimism. And medical science has long recognized the profound, instantaneous benefits of laughter on virtually every important organ in the human body. Even forced laughter reduces health-sapping tension while it simultaneously relaxes the muscles and exercises the organs. In fact, three minutes of sustained laughter will exercise your body as much as thirty minutes on a rowing machine.

Lighten up your outlook to relieve nervousness, tension, or fatigue. Indulge in a daily dose of laughter and discover its beneficial effects, both mentally and physically.

Attitude

[Jesus] said to them: "Truly I say to you, if you have faith as a mustard seed, you shall say to this mountain, 'Move from here to there,' and it shall move; and nothing shall be impossible to you."

Matthew 17:20 NAS

Faith comes by hearing, and hearing by the word of God.

Romans 10:17 NKJV

The boy's father exclaimed, "I do believe; help me overcome my unbelief!"

Mark 9:24

To have faith is to be sure of the things we hope for, to be certain of the things we cannot see.

Hebrews 11:1 TEV

Disappointment Can Breed Victory

When the University of Michigan played the University of Wisconsin in basketball early in the 1989 season, Michigan's Rumeal Robinson found himself at the foul line with just seconds left in the game. His team was trailing by one point, and Rumeal knew that if he could sink both shots, Michigan would win. Sadly, he missed both shots. Wisconsin upset the favored Michigan, and Rumeal went to the locker room feeling devastated and embarrassed.

His dejection, however, led to a positive move on his part. He determined to shoot 100 extra foul shots at the end of each practice for the rest of the season. And that's just what he did!

The moment came when Rumeal Robinson stepped to the foul line in yet another game, again with the opportunity to make two shots. This time the game was the NCAA finals! But Rumeal was prepared. *Swish* went the first shot . . . and *swish*, the second. Those two points gave Michigan the victory and the collegiate national championship for the season.

Have your ever felt embarrassed or devastated that something didn't turn out the way you anticipated? Don't give up. Look for a way to overcome your failure, and victory can be yours.

Comfort

Many are the sorrows of the wicked; but he who
trusts in the LORD, lovingkindness shall surround
him.

Psalm 32:10 NAS

Blessed are you who hunger now, for you will be
satisfied. Blessed are you who weep now, for you
will laugh.

Luke 6:21

The eyes of the LORD are on those who fear him,
on those whose hope is in his unfailing love.

Psalm 33:18

You are my hiding place; You shall preserve me
from trouble; You shall surround me with songs of
deliverance.

Psalm 32:7 NKJV

See God's Hand

Robert was upset when an avalanche crushed his family's mountain cabin. The avalanche destroyed in ten seconds what had taken them several years to build.

Months later, Robert attended a meeting with a colleague who had a cabin on the same mountain. On the day of the avalanche, the man's wife and children had left their cabin to head home. Before leaving, one of the man's sons had offered a prayer for a safe trip. As they drove down the middle of the narrow mountain road they met an oncoming car. The man's wife slammed on her brakes, but her car skidded sideways into a snow bank, blocking the road. The occupants of both vehicles were unhurt, but it took almost an hour to get the woman's car unstuck. All that time it blocked the other vehicle from passing on up the mountain and into the path of the avalanche. Robert's colleague then said, "The occupants of the other car, Robert, were your wife and son."

Be slow to judge devastating circumstances in your life. Ask God to show you His comforting hand in the situation. You'll see that He was there helping you all along.

Confusion

If you want to know what God wants you to do,
ask him, and he will gladly tell you, for he is
always ready to give a bountiful supply of wisdom
to all who ask him; he will not resent it.

James 1:5 TLB

God is not the author of confusion, but of peace.

1 Corinthians 14:33 KJV

The LORD will accomplish what concerns me; Thy
lovingkindness, O LORD, is everlasting.

Psalm 138:8 NAS

Call to Me, and I will answer you, and show you
great and mighty things, which you do not know.

Jeremiah 33:3 NKJV

Just One Tree

A young man was concerned about the uncertainty of his future and confused about which direction to take with his life. He sat quietly on a park bench, watching squirrels scamper among the trees. Suddenly, a squirrel jumped from one high tree to another, aiming for a limb so far out of reach that the leap looked like sheer suicide. Though the squirrel missed its mark, it landed safely, and seemingly unconcerned, on a branch several feet below. The squirrel then scampered upward to its original goal, and all was well.

An old man was sitting on the other end of the bench. "Funny thing," the man remarked. "I've seen hundreds of 'em jump like that. A lot of 'em miss, but I've never seen any hurt in trying." Then the man chuckled and added, "I guess they've got to risk something if they don't want to spend their lives in just one tree."

The young man thought, *A squirrel takes a chance—have I less nerve than a squirrel?* He made up his mind in that moment to take the risk he had been considering, and sure enough—he landed safer and higher than he had dared to imagine.

Break through confusion by taking a bold leap of faith!

Confusion

Trust the Lord completely; don't ever trust yourself. In everything you do, put God first, and he will direct you and crown your efforts with success.

Proverbs 3:5-6 TLB

I will instruct thee and teach thee in the way which thou shalt go: I will guide thee with mine eye.

Psalm 32:8 KJV

For where envy and self-seeking exist, confusion and every evil thing are there.

James 3:16 NKJV

Your ears will hear a word behind you, "This is the way, walk in it," whenever you turn to the right or to the left.

Isaiah 30:21 NAS

Following the Guide

Many years ago when Egyptian troops conquered the region of Nubia, a regiment of soldiers crossed the desert with an Arab guide. Their water rations were limited, and the soldiers were suffering from great thirst. Suddenly, a beautiful lake appeared on the horizon. The soldiers insisted that their guide take them to its banks. The guide knew the desert well and recognized that what they were seeing was just a mirage. He told the soldiers that the lake was not real and refused to lose precious time by wandering from the designated course.

Angry words followed. The soldiers decided they didn't need the guide's advice and parted company from him. Yet as the soldiers moved toward the lake, it receded into the distance. Finally, they recognized that the lake was only burning sand. Raging thirst and horrible despair engulfed them. Without their guide, they were lost and without water. Not one of them survived.

Be sure that what you seek today is not only within the realm of reality, but even more importantly, that it is part of God's plan for your life. Any other goal is likely to be unworthy of your pursuit, and may even be deadly.

Courage

Don't be afraid, for I am with you. Do not be dismayed, for I am your God. I will strengthen you. I will help you. I will uphold you with my victorious right hand.

Isaiah 41:10 NLT

Be strong, and let your heart take courage, all you who hope in the LORD.

Psalm 31:24 NAS

Be on your guard; stand firm in the faith; be men of courage; be strong.

1 Corinthians 16:13

The fear of man brings a snare, but whoever trusts in the LORD shall be safe.

Proverbs 29:25 NKJV

Tough Goals

After falling twice in the 1988 Olympic speedskating races, Dan Jansen sought out sports psychologist Dr. Jim Loehr, who helped Jansen focus on the mental aspects of skating and taught him how to balance sport and life. Coach Peter Mueller put Jansen through extremely strenuous workouts. When the 1994 Olympics arrived, Jansen had recently set a 500-meter world record and had more confidence than ever.

Though the 500-meter race seemed to be all his, inexplicably, Jansen fell. Dr. Loehr immediately advised Jansen to start preparing for the 1000-meter race and stop reliving the 500. The psychologist urged him to put the 500-meter race behind him and concentrate on what was ahead.

The 1000! For years Jansen had considered it his weaker event. Now it was his last chance for an Olympic medal. As the race began, Jansen said, "I just seemed to be sailing along." Though he slipped during the race and came within an inch of stepping on a lane marker, Jansen didn't panic. He raced on and recorded a world-record time that won him the gold medal!

Don't be intimidated by your own goals. Like Dan Jansen, your toughest goal may be linked to your greatest triumph.

Courage

Be very courageous to keep and to do all that is written in the Book of the Law of Moses, lest you turn aside from it to the right hand or to the left.
Joshua 23:6 NKJV

Be strong and courageous, do not be afraid or tremble . . . for the LORD your God is the one who goes with you. He will not fail you or forsake you.
Deuteronomy 31:6 NAS

The LORD is my light and my salvation—so why should I be afraid?
Psalm 27:1 NLT

Be strong and of a good courage; be not afraid, neither be thou dismayed: for the LORD thy God is with thee whithersoever thou goest.
Joshua 1:9 KJV

Love and Courage

One night during the Civil War, a stranger arrived at Henry Ward Beecher's home. Mrs. Beecher answered the knock at the door and found a tall and gangly stranger, asking to see the great preacher privately. He refused to give his name.

Because her husband's life had been threatened recently, Mrs. Beecher declined to receive him into their home and sent him away. She returned upstairs and told her husband about the stranger at the door and what she had done.

Beecher, who never seemed to know fear, descended at once and hurried after the man. He invited him back to his house and brought him inside, where he conversed with him privately for some time.

Later, when Beecher rejoined his wife, he told her what he had done. He also revealed that the muffled stranger had been none other than Abraham Lincoln, the President of the United States. He, too, was in a crisis and feeling threatened by evil. He came requesting prayer.

While we are never asked to openly defy common sense or to show disregard for our lives, the Lord does ask us to take risks in showing His love and sharing the Gospel with those in need. Love without courage is ineffective, but love with courage can change the world.

Dating

You are not to keep company with anyone who claims to be a brother Christian but indulges in sexual sins, or is greedy, or is a swindler, or worships idols, or is a drunkard, or abusive. Don't even eat lunch with such a person.

1 Corinthians 5:11 TLB

God wants you to be holy and to stay away from sexual sins. He wants each of you to learn to control your own body in a way that is holy and honorable.

1 Thessalonians 4:3-4 NCV

Keep company with the wise and you will become wise. If you make friends with stupid people, you will be ruined.

Proverbs 13:20 TEV

Walk in the way of good men, and keep to the paths of the righteous.

Proverbs 2:20 NAS

Consistent Character

A young man and his girlfriend found it hard to find time for special dates because of their busy schedules. The man decided that a casual picnic in the park would be relaxing and fun as well, so he and his girlfriend went into a fast-food restaurant and ordered a bag of chicken to go.

Moments earlier, the manager had placed the day's cash in a plain paper bag and set it at the side of the serving counter. Another clerk reached for the couple's chicken order and mistakenly gave them the bag of money. The couple paid for their order, got in their car, and drove to the park for their picnic. But when they opened the bag, they found that there were no drumsticks, only greenbacks!

After briefly discussing their find, they decided the right thing to do was to return the money. When they arrived at the restaurant, the manager was ecstatic. "I can't believe it!" he said. "You've got to be the two most honest people in this city."

Though their special date didn't turn out as planned, the man's integrity and honesty won his girlfriend's heart. Consistent strength of character is more important than occasional tokens of romance.

Dating

A man who is not married is busy with the Lord's work, trying to please the Lord. . . . A woman who is not married or a girl who has never married is busy with the Lord's work. She wants to be holy in body and spirit.

1 Corinthians 7:32,34 NCV

Do not stir up nor awaken love until it pleases.

Song of Solomon 2:7 NKJV

Do not be deceived: "Bad company corrupts good morals."

1 Corinthians 15:33 NAS

Do not be yoked together with unbelievers. For what do righteousness and wickedness have in common? Or what fellowship can light have with darkness?

2 Corinthians 6:14

Dates and Dreams

In 1928, a happy, ambitious young nursing student was diagnosed with tuberculosis. Her family sent her to a sanitarium in Saranac Lake for what they hoped would be only several months of "curing." However, Isabel Smith was destined to remain in bed for 21 years!

Most people may have given up, but not Isabel. She never ceased to pursue the art of living. She read voraciously, loved to write letters, and taught other patients to read and write.

While ill, Isabel met a kind gentleman who was also a patient at the sanitarium. They began to date as best they could within the walls of the sanitarium. They studied together, read to each other, and kept each other company. Isabel dreamed of marrying him one day and having a little house in the moutains. Finally, after her discharge from the sanitarium, they did marry. She then wrote a book about "all the *good* things life has brought me" and earned enough in royalties to buy her mountain retreat.

Isabel Smith achieved everything she set out to achieve, even when the odds against her were 1,000 to 1. Even flat on her back in bed, she never quit growing, learning, giving, and loving.

Death or Loss

We know that our body—the tent we live in here on earth—will be destroyed. But when that happens, God will have a house for us. . . . It will be a home in heaven that will last forever.

2 Corinthians 5:1 NCV

Blessed are those who mourn, for they shall be comforted.

Matthew 5:4 NKJV

He died for us so that, whether we are awake or asleep, we may live together with him.

1 Thessalonians 5:10

If the Spirit of God, who raised Jesus from death, lives in you, then he who raised Christ from death will also give life to your mortal bodies by the presence of his Spirit in you.

Romans 8:11 TEV

Strength in Others

In both fall and spring, geese can be seen migrating in a beautiful V-shaped formation. Scientists have discovered that the lead goose does the most work by breaking the force of the headwinds. At certain intervals, relative to the strength of the headwinds, the lead goose will drop back and take up a position at the end of the formation. A goose next to the former leader will take the lead spot in the "V."

Scientists have calculated that it takes up to 60 percent less effort for geese to fly this way. The flapping of all those wings creates an uplift of air. The uplift effect is greatest at the rear of the formation. In essence, the geese are taking turns "uplifting" one another. After a turn at the point of the "V," the lead goose is allowed to rest and be "carried" by the others, until it regains its strength and gradually moves forward in the formation to take its place in the lead role again.

When we face death or loss we need friends and family around us who can cooperate and work together. All can be "lifted up" when that happens. Is there someone today you can "uplift" with friendship, caring, or prayer?

Death or Loss

For I am convinced that nothing can ever separate
us from his love. Death can't, and life can't. . . .
Nothing will ever be able to separate us from the
love of God demonstrated by our Lord Jesus
Christ when he died for us.

Romans 8:38-39 TLB

Those who walk uprightly enter into peace; they
find rest as they lie in death.

Isaiah 57:2

Even when walking through the dark valley of
death I will not be afraid, for you are close beside
me, guarding, guiding all the way.

Psalm 23:4 TLB

If we live, it is for the LORD that we live, and if we
die, it is for the LORD that we die. So whether we
live or die, we belong to the LORD.

Romans 14:8 TEV

Keep On Keeping On

Opera star Marguerite Piazza was at the height of her career, married to a devoted husband, mother of six healthy children. Then her world seemed to turn upside down. Her husband died suddenly and soon after, a spot on her cheek was diagnosed as a deadly type of cancer. A disfiguring surgery to remove her cheek was her only hope for survival. The same day she received this distressing news, she was scheduled to sing to a sell-out audience. What would she do?

Marguerite says, "What can you do at a time like that? You do what you are paid to do, and I was paid to lift people with my talent." As she stood in the wings of the opera house, Marguerite prayed for the strength to keep going. She performed her heart out; no one in the audience was the wiser to her loss. Even after Marguerite had her surgery, she retained her beauty, raised her family, and continued to sing!

Though difficult times accompany death and loss, Marguerite sought God for the strength to keep on keeping on. Worry won't help. Misery won't bring you to the top. Facing each new day in God's strength is the only way.

Depression

In my great trouble I cried to the Lord and he answered me; from the depths of death I called, and Lord, you heard me!

Jonah 2:2 TLB

Answer me quickly, O LORD; my spirit fails. Do not hide your face from me or I will be like those who go down to the pit. Let the morning bring me word of your unfailing love, for I have put my trust in you. Show me the way I should go, for to you I lift up my soul.

Psalm 143:7-8

I will refresh the weary and satisfy the faint.

Jeremiah 31:25

The LORD also will be a refuge for the oppressed, a refuge in times of trouble.

Psalm 9:9 NKJV

Overcomers

In 1980 Mount Saint Helens erupted, and the Pacific Northwest shuddered under its devastating impact. Forests were destroyed by fire. Rivers were choked with debris. Fish and other wildlife died. Toxic fumes filled the air. Reporters ominously predicted that acid rain would develop from the ash-laden clouds. The future for the area seemed bleak.

Nevertheless, less than a year after the eruption, scientists discovered that despite the fact that the rivers had been clogged with hot mud, volcanic ash, and floating debris, some of the salmon and steelhead had managed to survive. By using alternate streams and waterways, some of which were less than six inches deep, the fish returned home to spawn.

Within a few short years, the fields, lakes, and rivers surrounding Mount Saint Helens teemed with life. The water and soil seemed to benefit from the nutrients supplied by the exploding volcano. Even the mountain itself began to show signs of new vegetation.

Challenges in life can enrich us and make us stronger. Trouble may only be the means to show you a different way to go, a different way to live. It may be an opportunity to start afresh. All of God's creation was designed to overcome!

Depression

We have troubles all around us, but we are not
defeated. We do not know what to do, but we do
not give up the hope of living. We are persecuted,
but God does not leave us. . . . So we do not
give up.

2 Corinthians 4:8-9,16 NCV

Cast your burden upon the LORD, and He will
sustain you; He will never allow the righteous to
be shaken.

Psalm 55:22 NAS

God is our refuge and strength, a tested help in
times of trouble.

Psalm 46:1 TLB

[Jesus said]: "In this world you will have trouble.
But take heart! I have overcome the world."

John 16:33

The Fog of Depression

On a cool morning in July of 1952, Florence Chadwick waded into the waters off of Catalina Island, intending to swim the channel to the California coast. Though an experienced long-distance swimmer, Florence knew this swim would be difficult. The water was numbingly cold, and the fog was so thick Florence could hardly see the boat that carried her trainer.

Florence swam for more than fifteen hours. Several times she could sense sharks swimming next to her in the inky waters. Rifles were fired from the trainer's boat to help keep the sharks at bay. Yet when Florence looked around her, all she could see was the fog. When she finally asked to be lifted from the water, she was only a half-mile from her goal. In a later interview Florence admitted that it wasn't the cold, fear, or exhaustion that caused her to fail in her attempt to swim the Catalina Channel. It was the fog.

The struggles we face can sometimes cloak us in a fog of depression. Remember, even if you can't see the end of your trouble, press on. God hasn't brought you this far to leave you. He is standing there just outside the fog waiting for your call.

Discouragement

My mouth would encourage you; comfort from
my lips would bring you relief.
Job 16:5

You are my hiding place from every storm of life;
you even keep me from getting into trouble! You
surround me with songs of victory.
Psalm 32:7 TLB

Those who know you, LORD, will trust you; you
do not abandon anyone who comes to you.
Psalm 9:10 TEV

When life is good, enjoy it. But when life is hard,
remember: God gives good times and hard times.
Ecclesiastes 7:14 NCV

Trying Again for Victory

When David Yudovin entered the 64 degree water before dawn, he was trying to complete a journey he had begun nearly twenty years before. In 1978, only 250 yards from the end of a marathon swim near Ventura, California, Yudovin had a near-fatal heart attack. He fought his way back to health and finally, at age forty-five, Yudovin felt ready to take on his supreme challenge, swimming the English Channel.

The odds against a successful channel swim are great. Yudovin had tried three other times and failed. The channel is often laced with sewage, oil slicks, seaweed, jellyfish, and up to four hundred ships a day. Yet the lure of that dangerous twenty-one-plus mile stretch of water never left him.

On August 20, 1996, the weather reports indicated it was now or never. So Yudovin swam. Eight hours into his marathon, a storm cell bore down on him, producing hard rain, strong tides, and choppy water. But Yudovin continued on. When he climbed out of the water near Calais, France, he was elated. "It's so rewarding and so fulfilling it almost tickles inside," he said.

Yudovin faced his discouragement head on. His fourth attempt was a victory! Is it time for you to try again?

Discouragement

Behold, the eye of the LORD is on those who fear Him, on those who hope in His mercy.

Psalm 33:18 NKJV

The LORD God is a sun and shield: the LORD will give grace and glory: no good thing will he withhold from them that walk uprightly.

Psalm 84:11 KJV

May our LORD Jesus Christ Himself and God our Father, who has loved us and given us eternal comfort and good hope by grace, comfort and strengthen your hearts in every good work and word.

2 Thessalonians 2:16-17 NAS

Trust in Him at all times, you people; pour out your heart before Him; God is a refuge for us.

Psalm 62:8 NKJV

One More Time

Moses easily could have been discouraged and given up. He lived with a foster family, had a strong temper, a stammering tongue, and a crime record. Yet when God called to him, he said, "Yes."

Joshua had visited the promised land and then been forced to wander in a wilderness for 40 years with cowards who didn't believe, as he did, that they could possess the land. He could have given up in discouragement, but he didn't. He was willing to wait and go when and where God said to go.

Peter had a hard time making the transition from fisherman to fisher of men. He sank while trying to walk on water, was strongly rebuked by Jesus for trying to tell Him what to do, and denied knowing Jesus in the very hour Jesus needed him most. He easily could have floundered in a sea of despair. But when the opportunity came to preach before thousands on the Day of Pentecost, Peter responded.

Each of these men could have allowed their discouragement to hold them back. Yet each one chose to persevere. These heroes of the faith realized that the way to overcome discouragement is to get up just one more time than you fall down!

Discouragement

All people will hate you because you follow me, but those people who keep their faith until the end will be saved.

Matthew 10:22 NCV

If we are faithful to the end, trusting God just as firmly as when we first believed, we will share in all that belongs to Christ.

Hebrews 3:14 NLT

Encourage God's people to endure patiently every trial and persecution, for they are his saints who remain firm to the end in obedience to his commands.

Revelation 14:12 TLB

When your faith is tested, your endurance has a chance to grow.

James 1:3 NLT

Don't Give Up

In the 1700s, an English cobbler kept a map of the world on his workshop wall so that he might be reminded to pray for the nations of the world. As the result of such prayer, he became especially burdened for a specific missionary outreach. He shared this burden at a meeting of ministers, but was told by a senior minister, "Young man, sit down. When God wants to convert the heathen, He will do it without your help or mine."

The cobbler, William Carey, did not let this man's remarks put out the flame of his concern. When he couldn't find others to support the missionary cause that burdened his soul, he became a missionary himself. His legendary pioneering efforts and mighty exploits for God in India are well recorded.

Be careful in how you respond to the enthusiasm of others, that you don't dampen a zeal for God. Be cautious in how you respond to the new ideas of another, that you don't squelch God-given creativity. Be generous and kind in evaluating the work of others, so that you might encourage those things which are worthy. Be slow to judge and quick to praise. And, pray for the same in your own life!

Doubt

[Jesus said]: "Stop your doubting, and believe!"
John 20:27 TEV

God has said, "I will never, *never* fail you nor
forsake you."
Hebrews 13:5 TLB

Jesus answered . . . "Truly I say to you, whoever
says to this mountain, 'Be taken up and cast into
the sea,' and does not doubt in his heart, but
believes that what he says is going to happen, it
shall be *granted* him."
Mark 11:22,23 NAS

Why are you downcast, O my soul? Why so
disturbed within me? Put your hope in God, for I
will yet praise him, my Savior and my God.
Psalm 42:11

One in a Hundred

Tommy John was the leading pitcher in the National League in 1974. His team was on its way to the World Series. But during a game in September, Tommy ruptured a ligament in his elbow. When he asked his surgeon if he had any chance of pitching again, he was told, "The odds are one in a hundred."

Shortly after his operation and with his arm in a cast, Tommy and his family went to church. The sermon that morning was about Abraham and Sarah and the child that was born when they were well advanced in years. The minister looked right at Tommy as he said, "You know, with God, nothing is impossible."

That was all Tommy needed to hear. Praying for God's strength, Tommy began the daily work of rehabilitation. His progress was slow — it was a great victory when he could finally bend his little finger to touch his thumb. Finally, after eighteen months of this painful process, Tommy John walked back onto the pitcher's mound, eventually pitching more games after his surgery than before.

Today, choose to look to the Source of your strength. No matter what odds the world gives you, with Him, all things are possible.

Doubt

The one who doubts is like the surf of the sea driven and tossed by the wind.

James 1:6 NAS

Let us hold firmly to the hope that we have confessed, because we can trust God to do what he promised.

Hebrews 10:23 NCV

Jesus said . . . "If you have faith as a mustard seed, you will say to this mountain, 'Move from here to there,' and it will move; and nothing will be impossible for you."

Matthew 17:20 NKJV

Be merciful to those who doubt; snatch others from the fire and save them.

Jude 22-23

Doubt Not

In May of 1996, Los Angeles Dodger Brett Butler checked into the hospital for what he thought would be a simple tonsillectomy. However, the surgeons found that he had cancer. The news hit Butler hard. His mother had died of cancer a year before. Now it seemed to Butler that though he was only thirty-eight years old, he too faced death. But after the initial shock wore off, Butler chose to respond with faith instead of doubt. He underwent two operations and thirty-two radiation treatments, determined to return to the Dodgers lineup.

Few believed he could do it, but Butler did not doubt. Butler said, "I believe God answers prayer. I want to acknowledge that in some capacity. This is an opportunity to show I am a disciple for Jesus. Now I'll be able to measure my success from the lowness of my career."

Finally, on September sixth, Butler was once again in uniform on the ball field. Because of his faith and persistence, Butler scored a run and fielded two nice catches to help his team win the game.

Though the events in your life may seem overwhelming, respond in faith instead of doubt and watch God turn those struggles into opportunities for your success.

Drugs/Alcohol

Be not drunk with wine, wherein is excess; but be filled with the Spirit.

Ephesians 5:18 KJV

Those who sleep, sleep at night, and those who get drunk, get drunk at night. But since we belong to the day, let us be self-controlled.

1 Thessalonians 5:7-8

The wrong things the sinful self does are clear . . . feeling envy, being drunk, having wild and wasteful parties, and doing other things like these.

Galatians 5:19,21 NCV

Let us conduct ourselves properly, as people who live in the light of day—no orgies or drunkenness, no immorality or indecency, no fighting or jealousy.

Romans 13:13 TEV

Present-day Reality, or Truth

Stephen R. Covey once spoke to a large group of college students on the subject of the "new morality." He asserted that there are principles in this world that should be respected and adhered to, no matter how much you believe in personal freedom.

One student contended there was no right or wrong in a particular situation; it was a matter of interpretation. Not so, said Covey. Anytime you violate a fundamental principle, there's a price to be paid. By the look on the students' faces, however, Covey knew they believed he was out of touch with present-day reality.

Covey suggested an experiment. "Each of you knows in your heart what the truth is," he said. "Sit quietly for a minute. Ask yourself what the truth is concerning this situation."

At the end of the minute, several of the students admitted that they weren't quite so sure of themselves anymore. One young man even said he had changed his mind completely. Their encounter with truth shattered their "present-day reality." Before you are tempted to give in to the voice of the crowd, let God speak quietly to your heart, and pay attention to the still, small voice of truth.

Drugs or Alcohol

Woe to those who rise early in the morning that they may pursue strong drink; who stay up late in the evening that wine may inflame them! . . . They do not pay attention to the deeds of the LORD, nor do they consider the work of His hands.

Isaiah 5:11-12 NAS

Don't let the sparkle and the smooth taste of strong wine deceive you. For in the end it bites like a poisonous serpent.

Proverbs 23:31-32 TLB

Wine is a mocker and beer a brawler; whoever is led astray by them is not wise.

Proverbs 20:1

Those who live according to the flesh set their minds on the things of the flesh, but those who live according to the Spirit, the things of the Spirit.

Romans 8:5 NKJV

Change Your Hitching Post

A farmer in the old west had a reputation for frequenting the local bar. Then, he was converted to Christ. Whenever he visited town, however, he continued to tie his horse to the bar's hitching post.

One day, an elderly deacon from the church kindly said to the younger man, "Pardon me if I make a suggestion from my experience. No matter how strong you think you are, take my advice and change your hitching post."

Changing your "hitching post" is an important part of one's Christian witness. Consider the story of a couple from a sophisticated urban area. They had been part of a social set in which alcohol freely flowed. After they were converted, they discovered that when they tried to witness, they were highly ineffective as long as they were holding glasses in their hands, even if their glasses contained a soft drink. When they switched to holding coffee cups, however, people noticed not only the change in their cups but in the rest of their behavior and were more willing to listen to their testimony.

When you proclaim Christ's influence in your life, people expect to see a difference in how you act. Do you need to change your "hitching post"?

Failure

I am very happy to brag about my weaknesses. Then Christ's power can live in me.

2 Corinthians 12:9 NCV

Our High Priest is not one who cannot feel sympathy for our weaknesses. . . . Let us have confidence, then, and approach God's throne, where there is grace. There we will receive mercy and find grace to help us just when we need it.

Hebrews 4:15-16 TEV

If we believe not, yet he abideth faithful: he cannot deny himself.

2 Timothy 2:13 KJV

Plans go wrong for lack of advice; many counselors bring success.

Proverbs 15:22 NLT

Listen and Learn From Failure

Richard Carlyle was a young, aggressive salesman who skyrocketed to the position of national sales manager by the time he was thirty. Soon after, however, a bad economic turn caused his company some sudden reverses. Pressure to produce mounted, but Carlyle found that his inexperience prevented him from doing the job required of him. He went to upper management, admitted that he was in over his head, and suggested that he be permitted to find someone to come into the company over him. He offered to either work with the person or resign.

Appreciating his candor and recognizing his potential, Carlyle's bosses went along with his suggestion. They hired a retired, experienced sales manager and gave him a two-year contract. With coaching from this older, more experienced man, Carlyle acquired the necessary know-how to successfully run the department once again.

Richard Carlyle neither denied his failure, nor did he let it demoralize him. He viewed his failure as a sign of inexperience and addressed the issue constructively. Our failures often send us messages about things that we may need to do or not do. We are wise to listen and learn when necessary, for failure can be a wise teacher.

Failure

Though I walk in the midst of trouble, You will revive me; You will stretch out Your hand against the wrath of my enemies, and Your right hand will save me.

Psalm 138:7 NKJV

The LORD is good, a stronghold in the day of trouble, and He knows those who take refuge in Him.

Nahum 1:7 NAS

When thou passest through the waters, I will be with thee; and through the rivers, they shall not overflow thee: when thou walkest through the fire, thou shalt not be burned; neither shall the flame kindle upon thee. For I am the LORD thy God.

Isaiah 43:2-3 KJV

Do not be afraid or discouraged, for the LORD God, my God, is with you. He will not fail you or forsake you.

1 Chronicles 28:20

Reason to Hope

He had been expelled from college and his business attempts had failed. Now, as he stood on the windswept shores of Lake Michigan one wintry night, the 32-year-old took one last look at the sky above him as he prepared to cast himself into the freezing water.

It was an overpowering moment. He felt a rush of awe as he saw the starry heavens and the thought seared his mind, *You have no right to eliminate yourself. You do not belong to you.* R. Buckminster Fuller walked away from the lake and started over.

From that point on, he embarked on a journey that led him into careers as an inventor, engineer, mathematician, architect, poet, and cosmologist. He eventually won dozens of honorary degrees and a Nobel Prize nomination. Fuller wrote two dozen books, circled the globe 57 times, and told millions about his dreams for the future.

The day Buckminster Fuller encountered hope was the day he began to find meaning for his life. There is always a reason to hope. Hope gives us the strength to walk away from failure and move on to success.

Family

Choose for yourselves this day whom you will serve. . . . But as for me and my house, we will serve the LORD.

Joshua 24:15 NKJV

Be ye kind one to another, tenderhearted, forgiving one another, even as God for Christ's sake hath forgiven you.

Ephesians 4:32 KJV

Teach a child to choose the right path, and when he is older he will remain upon it.

Proverbs 22:6 TLB

Children, obey your parents in the Lord, for this is right. "Honor your father and mother"—which is the first commandment with a promise—"that it may go well with you and that you may enjoy long life on the earth."

Ephesians 6:1-3

Your Family Name

Armstrong Williams liked nothing better than to be sent on errands in the family pickup, but this time his spirits were dampened. His father had sent him to the store to buy wire and fencing for their farm and had told him to ask for credit. The young man feared what might happen. He had seen other black friends ask for credit and then stand with their heads down, while the store owner questioned their ability to repay.

When Armstrong took his purchases to the register, he said cautiously, "I need to put this on credit." A farmer standing next to him sneered at him. But the shopkeeper's face held no ill will. "Sure," he said easily. "You're one of James Williams' sons. Your daddy is always good for it."

Armstrong was filled with pride. James Williams' son. Those three words had opened a door to an adult's respect. That day Armstrong discovered that a good name could carry with it a capital of good will and that keeping the good name of his family was an important, lifelong responsibility. Regardless of background, environment, or education, everyone has the same opportunity to create a good reputation—and keep it.

Family

He will direct his children and his household after him to keep the way of the LORD by doing what is right and just.

Genesis 18:19

They said, "Believe in the Lord Jesus, and you shall be saved, you and your household."

Acts 16:31 NAS

I, the Lord God . . . declare . . . "I will honor only those who honor me, and I will despise those who despise me."

1 Samuel 2:30 TLB

If someone does not know how to lead the family, how can that person take care of God's church?

1 Timothy 3:5 NCV

Giving and Taking Responsibility

Wilson Harrell recalls that his father made him a cotton buyer at his gin when Wilson was only 11 years old. It was an awesome responsibility for a young boy. He would cut open a bale, pull out a wad, examine the sample, identify the grade, and set the price. The first farmer he faced called Wilson's father over and said, "I've worked too hard to have an 11-year-old boy decide what I'll live on next year."

The elder Mr. Harrell was a man of few words and merely replied, "His grade stands." Over the years, Wilson's father always publicly backed his son's grade. However, when they were alone, Mr. Harrell would double-check any of the questionable bundles. If Wilson had paid too little by undergrading, the boy had to go to the farmer, tell him of the mistake, and pay him the difference. If he'd paid too much, Mr. Harrell didn't say a word.

Learning responsibility within the confines of a family can be a means to growth and honesty. Wilson Harrell says, "My father understood an awful lot about making a man out of a boy. He gave me responsibility and then backed my hand." Does someone in your family need you to stand by them today?

Fear

Do not be afraid—I am with you! I am your God—let nothing terrify you! I will make you strong and help you; I will protect you and save you.

Isaiah 41:10 TEV

Don't fear, little flock, because your Father wants to give you the kingdom.

Luke 12:32 NCV

Let us be bold, then, and say, "The LORD is my helper, I will not be afraid. What can anyone do to me?"

Hebrews 13:6 TEV

The LORD will give strength unto his people; the LORD will bless his people with peace.

Psalm 29:11 KJV

Obstacles are Opportunities

Workmen hired to build a bridge across a river needed to get an iron cable from one side of the river to the other, yet the river was too swift to cross by boat and too wide to throw the cable across.

An engineer decided to send a kite over the river to the opposite shore. Attached to the kite was a very light string. Once the kite was in the hands of workmen on the far side of the river, the engineer attached a lightweight rope to his end of the original kite string. The workmen on the far side of the river pulled the kite string all the way across the river, dragging the lightweight rope along with it. The engineer then attached a heavier rope and instructed the workmen to pull this across the river too. He continued increasing the weights of the attachments until he finally attached a cable strong enough to pull the bridge's iron cable across the river.

Don't let the obstacle of fear stop you in your tracks. Faith lets you move forward when you believe that God can and will help you. Link your faith with prayer, patience, and persistence, and you will be able to tackle any problem!

Fear

My flesh and my heart may fail, but God is the strength of my heart and my portion forever.

Psalm 73:26 NAS

In the day of my trouble I will call upon You, for You will answer me.

Psalm 86:7 NKJV

Do not fear, for those who are with us are more than those who are with them.

2 Kings 6:16 NAS

God hath not given us the spirit of fear; but of power, and of love, and of a sound mind.

2 Timothy 1:7 KJV

Hang on to Hope

When Christopher Columbus set sail to discover a new route to the Indies, he truly believed that he could and would reach his destination. He had accumulated evidence for years that convinced him he would find land on an opposite shore if he sailed west from Europe. Even though other explorers had abandoned their voyages in fear of sailing off the edge of the world, Columbus felt they had quit too soon.

However, Columbus hired sailors who did not completely share his belief in a far off western land. After weeks of sailing with no land in sight, the sailors were fearful and on the verge of mutiny. But Columbus saw an encouraging sign on the ocean swells—a small tree branch. The branches' leaves were green, indicating that land could not be far away. The branch gave the sailors a burst of enthusiasm and a renewed hope. Not long after its discovery, the sailor in the crow's nest rang out the cry that thrilled all their hearts, "Land! Land ahead!"

Fear tempted the sailors to abandon not only their journey, but to abandon their hope, too. Hang on to your hope and enthusiasm, and you will conquer your fear.

Forgiveness

Let the wicked leave their way of life and change their way of thinking. Let them turn to the LORD, our God; he is merciful and quick to forgive.

Isaiah 55:7 TEV

"Come now, and let us reason together," says the LORD, "Though your sins are as scarlet, they will be as white as snow; though they are red like crimson, they will be like wool."

Isaiah 1:18 NAS

Blessed is he whose transgressions are forgiven, whose sins are covered.

Psalm 32:1

Be kind to each other, tenderhearted, forgiving one another, just as God has forgiven you because you belong to Christ.

Ephesians 4:32 TLB

A Testimony of Forgiveness

Jewish physician Boris Kornfeld was imprisoned in a Siberian labor camp. He worked in surgery, helping both the staff and prisoners. While there, Dr. Kornfeld met a Christian whose quiet faith and frequent recitation of the Lord's Prayer moved him.

Once, while repairing a guard's slashed artery, Dr. Kornfeld considered lightly suturing the artery so that the guard would slowly bleed to death internally. Immediately the horror of such an act appalled him, and he prayed, "Forgive us our sins as we forgive those who sin against us." After this experience, Dr. Kornfeld refused to obey the inhumane prison rules, even though his rebellion endangered his life.

One day Dr. Kornfeld examined a patient who had undergone cancer surgery. The man's eyes reflected a deep spiritual misery that Dr. Kornfeld recognized. He shared his story with the man, including a confession of his secret faith. Though Dr. Kornfeld was murdered that night as he slept, his testimony of forgiveness convinced his patient to become a Christian. The patient survived the Siberian labor camp, eventually writing a book about it. That patient was Aleksandr Solzhenitsyn.

By practicing a life of forgiveness, a nameless Christian ultimately changed the world with his witness. Are you living a life of forgiveness today?

Forgiveness

If we confess our sins, he is faithful and just to forgive us our sins, and to cleanse us from all unrighteousness.

1 John 1:9 KJV

You, Lord, are good, and ready to forgive, and abundant in mercy to all those who call upon You.

Psalm 86:5 NKJV

[The LORD declares]: "I am the One who forgives all your sins, for my sake; I will not remember your sins."

Isaiah 43:25 NCV

If my people will humble themselves and pray, and search for me, and turn from their wicked ways, I will hear them from heaven and forgive their sins and heal their land.

2 Chronicles 7:14 TLB

Shake Hands

Laura Ingalls Wilder once had an old dog, Shep. As he grew older, Shep's eyesight became poor, and he didn't always recognize friends. Wilder writes, "Once he made a mistake and barked savagely at an old friend whom he really regarded as one of the family, though he had not seen him for some time. Later, as we all sat in the yard, Shep seemed uneasy. At last he walked deliberately to the visitor, sat up, and held out his paw. It was so plainly an apology that our friend said, 'That's all right, Shep, old fellow! Shake and forget it!' Shep shook hands and walked away perfectly satisfied."

Harboring a grudge or remembering a slight or injustice will only bring the hard shell of bitterness to your heart. Yet people are often quicker to judge than they are to forgive. Unresolved bitterness and failure to forgive will not only destroy relationships but will also elevate your blood pressure, increase the risk of stroke, cause myriad aches and pains, and affect your ability to get a good night's sleep.

Is there an apology you need to make today or an offer of forgiveness you need to extend? Then shake hands, forgive, and forget. You'll be glad you did.

Friendship

A friend loveth at all times.

Proverbs 17:17 KJV

[Jesus said]: "No longer do I call you servants, for a servant does not know what his master is doing; but I have called you friends, for all things that I heard from My Father I have made known to you."

John 15:15 NKJV

Two are better than one, because they have a good return for their work: If one falls down, his friend can help him up.

Ecclesiastes 4:9-10

A man of many friends comes to ruin, but there is a friend who sticks closer than a brother.

Proverbs 18:24 NAS

Reach Out in Friendship

More than 95 percent of all Americans receive at least one Christmas card each year. The average is actually more than seventy cards per family! Millions of cards are mailed each holiday season throughout the world. Have you ever wondered where this custom originated?

A museum director in the mid-19th century liked to send yearly notes to his friends at Christmastime, just to wish them a joyful holiday season. One year, he found he had little time to write. Yet he still wanted to send a message of good cheer. He asked his friend, John Horsely, to design a card that he might sign and send. Those who received the cards loved the idea and created cards of their own. And thus, the Christmas card was invented!

It's often the simple, heartfelt gestures in life that speak most loudly of friendship. Ask yourself today, *What can I do to bring a smile to the face of a friend? What can I do to bring good cheer into the life of a friend who is needy, troubled, sick, or sorrowing?* Follow through on your inspiration and remember, it's not a gift you are giving as much as a friendship you are building!

Friendship

"Abraham believed God, and it was credited to him as righteousness," and he was called God's friend.

James 2:23

Wounds from a friend are better than kisses from an enemy!

Proverbs 27:6 TLB

The greatest love you can have for your friends is to give your life for them. And you are my friends if you do what I command you.

John 15:13-14 TEV

The sweet smell of perfume and oils is pleasant, and so is good advice from a friend.

Proverbs 27:9 NCV

Friends Make Friends

The complex shapes of snowflakes have confounded scientists for centuries. In the past, scientists believed that the making of a snowflake was a two-step process. They believed that inside the winds of a winter storm a microscopic speck of dust would become trapped in a molecule of water vapor. Scientists suggested that this particle would then become heavily frosted with droplets of super-cooled water and plunge to earth. During its descent, the varying temperature and humidity would sculpt the heavy, icy crystal into a lacy snowflake. Or at least that's what scientists used to believe.

In recent decades, the true formation of the snowflake was discovered. Very few snowflakes actually contain dust or other particles. Dr. John Hallett of the University of Nevada discovered that the majority of snowflakes are formed from fragments of other snowflakes. As snowflakes are formed, extremely dry or cold air causes them to break up into smaller parts. The small fragments then act as seeds for new snowflakes to develop. Most of snow is made, therefore, by snow!

In like manner, friendly people generate friends. Their neighborly outlook inspires others to reach out and be friendly too. Pass along the seed of friendship and watch what develops in your own life.

Frustration

Call to Me, and I will answer you, and show you great and mighty things, which you do not know.
Jeremiah 33:3 NKJV

We know that all things work together for good to them that love God, to them who are the called according to his purpose.
Romans 8:28 KJV

Encourage the exhausted, and strengthen the feeble. Say to those with anxious heart, "Take courage, fear not. Behold, your God will come."
Isaiah 35:3-4 NAS

God is faithful; he will not let you be tempted beyond what you can bear. But when you are tempted, he will also provide a way out so that you can stand up under it.
1 Corinthians 10:13

Getting Somewhere

A frustrated young man once approached a successful businessman. "Success completely eludes me," he said. "I want to get somewhere in life."

"That's great!" the successful man replied. "And exactly where do you want to go?"

The young man's reply was inconclusive. "Well, I don't know for sure. But I'm not happy with the way things are."

The successful man probed, "What can you do best? What skills do you have? What do you think you're cut out for?"

The young man pondered the question and then replied, "I don't believe I have any particular skills. But I think I'm entitled to a better break."

The successful man tried a third time, "All right then. What would you *like* to do if you could have any job you wanted?" The young man's answer was vague and uncertain once again.

Finally the successful man advised, "Young man, you will always be frustrated. If you don't know where you want to go, how will you ever know when you have arrived?"

To alleviate frustration in your life, fix your sights on a specific destination or goal. Sharpen and clarify it. Then, take the steps necessary to begin to move toward your goal, rather than a vague "somewhere."

Frustration

The LORD says, "My thoughts are not like your thoughts. Your ways are not like my ways."
Isaiah 55:8 NCV

If God is on our side, who can ever be against us? Since he did not spare even his own Son for us but gave him up for us all, won't he also surely give us everything else?
Romans 8:31-32 TLB

I will make an eternal covenant with them. I will never stop doing good things for them, and I will make them fear me with all their heart, so that they will never turn away from me.
Jeremiah 32:40 TEV

Though I walk in the midst of trouble, You will revive me; You will stretch out Your hand against the wrath of my enemies, and Your right hand will save me. The LORD will perfect that which concerns me.
Psalm 138:7-8 NKJV

Going God's Way

There is no greater guarantee of frustration than trying to make your life fulfill a plan that God never intended. Antonio Salieri, an ambitious, but mediocre 18th-century composer offers this prayer in the film *Amadeus*:

"Lord, make me a great composer. Let me celebrate Your glory through music. And be celebrated myself. Make me famous through the world, dear God, make me immortal. After I die, let people speak my name forever with love for what I wrote. In return I will give You my chastity, my industry, my deep humility, my life."

When it became obvious to the superficially pious Salieri that he would never be as gifted as Wolfgang Amadeus Mozart, Salieri's life became fraught with jealousy and frustration. He plotted to destroy Mozart and turned away from God, convinced that God had betrayed him.

Whenever you feel unfulfilled or frustrated in an attempt to achieve a goal or position, make sure that you are going God's way and following God's plan. Legislating how God will use you, even in a great work for Him, will result in frustration rather than the satisfaction found in allowing Him to plan the way, the means, and the use of our lives in any way He desires, for His glory.

Giving

Let us stop going over the same old ground again and again, always teaching those first lessons about Christ. Let us go on instead to other things and become mature in our understanding, as strong Christians ought to be.

Hebrews 6:1 TLB

Practice these things and devote yourself to them, in order that your progress may be seen by all.

1 Timothy 4:15 TEV

Study to shew thyself approved unto God, a workman that needeth not to be ashamed, rightly dividing the word of truth.

2 Timothy 2:15 KJV

Open my eyes to see the wonderful truths in your law.

Psalm 119:18 NLT

Honeycomb Givers

There are three kinds of givers: the flint, the sponge, and the honeycomb. Which kind are you?

To get anything from the flint, you must hammer it. Yet, all you generally get are chips and sparks. The flint gives nothing away if it can help it, and even then only with a great display.

To get anything from the sponge, you must squeeze it. It readily yields to pressure, and the more it is pressed, the more it gives. Still, one must push.

To get anything from the honeycomb, however, one must only take what freely flows from it. It gives its sweetness generously, dripping on all without pressure, without begging or badgering.

Note too, that there is another difference in the honeycomb. It is a renewable resource. Unlike the flint or sponge, the honeycomb is connected to life; it is the product of the ongoing work and creative energy of bees.

If you are a "honeycomb giver" your life will be continually replenished and grow as you give. And, as long as you are connected to the Source of all life, you can never run dry. When you give freely you will receive in like manner, so that whatever you give away will soon be multiplied back to you.

Gossip

A gossip goes around revealing secrets, but those who are trustworthy can keep a confidence.

Proverbs 11:13 NLT

Don't gossip. Don't falsely accuse your neighbor of some crime, for I am Jehovah.

Leviticus 19:16 TLB

Men will be lovers of self, lovers of money, boastful, arrogant, revilers, disobedient to parents, ungrateful, unholy, unloving, irreconcilable, malicious gossips, without self-control.

2 Timothy 3:2-3 NAS

Without wood, a fire goes out; without gossip, quarreling stops.

Proverbs 26:20 TEV

Face to Face

A Christian man once heard a rumor that another Christian was speaking against him. He went to him and said, "Will you be kind enough to tell my faults to my face, that I may try to get rid of them?"

The other man agreed to do so. The first man continued, "Before you tell me what you think wrong in me, will you pray with me that my eyes may be opened to see my faults as you cite them?"

The second man prayed that God would open the eyes of his friend, and when he was finished, the first man said, "Please proceed with your complaints."

The second man quietly replied, "After praying over it, it looks that I have been serving the devil myself, and have need that you forgive me the wrong I have done in gossiping against you."

Several things are noteworthy: speak the truth to another person with love, seek the truth from one who will be honest with you, and do not include a third party in the exchange, for this is gossip. In speaking the truth, we often hear what we need to hear—from our own lips. In seeking the truth and refraining from gossip, we often gain a friend.

Gossip

No one who gossips can be trusted with a secret, but you can put confidence in someone who is trustworthy.

Proverbs 11:13 TEV

They have become filled with every kind of wickedness, evil, greed and depravity. They are full of envy, murder, strife, deceit and malice. They are gossips . . . those who do such things deserve death.

Romans 1:29,32

Gossips can't keep secrets, so avoid people who talk too much.

Proverbs 20:19 NCV

Women must likewise be dignified, not malicious gossips, but temperate, faithful in all things.

1 Timothy 3:11 NAS

Phony Friends

Joan Aho Ryan went shopping in a local mall with her mother. While there, the ladies ran into two women who lived in their neighborhood. Effusive greetings were exchanged, and then the ladies parted company. "What phonies," Joan's mother remarked when the other women were well out of earshot.

Her daughter asked her what she meant. Her mother explained, with obvious disdain, that she had sat at the swimming pool on several occasions with those two women and another friend, Sylvia. One day, she said, she sat with them and heard the three women discussing Sylvia's daughter's wedding reception that had taken place the week before. The two women raved about the food, the flowers, the elegant country club location, and the beautiful bride.

The older woman shook her head as she spoke, "When Sylvia left the table, however, you should have heard those two. I couldn't believe friends could be that two-faced. They ripped her apart, talking about how cheap she was, her homely son-in-law, the music they couldn't dance to. It was awful. And they call themselves friends," she clucked. "Who needs gossipy friends like that?"

Speaking well of others is not only a good way to acquire friends, but to keep them.

Guidance

Ask the LORD to bless your plans, and you will be successful in carrying them out.

Proverbs 16:3 TEV

I will instruct you (says the Lord) and guide you along the best pathway for your life; I will advise you and watch your progress.

Psalm 32:8 TLB

Only the LORD gives wisdom; he gives knowledge and understanding.

Proverbs 2:6 NCV

Thus says the LORD: "Stand in the ways and see, and ask for the old paths, where the good way is, and walk in it; then you will find rest for your souls."

Jeremiah 6:16 NKJV

I Am the Path

E. Stanley Jones tells the story of a missionary who became lost in an African jungle. Looking around, he saw nothing but bush and a few clearings. He stumbled about until he finally came across a native hut. He asked one of the natives if he could lead him out of the jungle and back to the mission station. The native agreed to help him.

The missionary thanked him profusely and asked, "Which way do we go?" The native replied, "This way. We must walk." And so they did, hacking their way through the unmarked jungle for more than an hour.

In pausing to rest, the missionary looked around and had the same overwhelming sense that he was lost. All he saw was bush, and a few clearings. "Are you quite sure this is the way?" he asked. "I don't see any path."

His guide looked at him and replied, "In this place, *I am* the path."

As we traverse life's jungles we also have an all-wise guide—God. When we have no clue about the way to go, God reminds us that He is our path, He is our guide. All we have to do is ask, "Which way do we go?"

Guidance

This God is our God for ever and ever; he will be our guide even to the end.

Psalm 48:14

The LORD will continually guide you, and satisfy your desire in scorched places, and give strength to your bones; and you will be like a watered garden, and like a spring of water whose waters do not fail.

Isaiah 58:11 NAS

Trust in the LORD with all thine heart; and lean not unto thine own understanding. In all thy ways acknowledge him, and he shall direct thy paths.

Proverbs 3:5-6 KJV

Show me your ways, O LORD, teach me your paths; guide me in your truth and teach me.

Psalm 25:4-5

Watch What You Catch

A dog once lived near the railroad tracks. He watched the freight trains roar past his dog house every day. One day the dog decided to chase one of the freight trains and catch it. He waited until the train slowed for a sharp curve and then boldly positioned himself in the middle of the tracks. The big freight train came to screeching halt only inches in front of the dog.

Once the dog had succeeded in stopping the train, he didn't know what to do with it. The engineer and brakeman yelled at him as they shooed him from the tracks and resumed their journey. In the end, "catching" the train didn't bring the dog the satisfaction he had thought it would. He probably would have been more fulfilled if he had chased and caught a rabbit.

Today, make sure that what you are pursuing is truly what you want, should you attain it. Though you may face difficulty or adverse circumstances in attaining your goal, don't despair. Ask for guidance, solicit advice, and persevere only if you can do so without compromising your values or identity. Only then will your direction be sure and your achievement fulfilling.

Impure Thoughts

Set your mind on things above, not on things on the earth.

Colossians 3:2 NKJV

Jesus [said to] Peter . . . "You are a dangerous trap to me. You are thinking merely from a human point of view, and not from God's."

Matthew 16:23 TLB

We pull down every proud obstacle that is raised against the knowledge of God; we take every thought captive and make it obey Christ.

2 Corinthians 10:5 TEV

The thoughts of the wicked are an abomination to the LORD: but the words of the pure are pleasant words.

Proverbs 15:26 KJV

Thinking and Doing

During the national spelling bee in Washington, D.C., eleven-year-old Rosalie Elliot, a champion from South Carolina, was asked to spell the word *avowal*. Her soft Southern accent made it difficult for the judges to determine if she had used an *a* or an *e* in the last syllable of the word. The judges deliberated for several minutes and listened to taped playbacks, but still they couldn't determine which letter had been used. Finally the chief judge asked Rosalie, "Was the letter an *a* or an *e*?"

Rosalie knew by now the correct spelling of the word and realized that she had misspelled the word. If she lied, she could continue; if she told the truth, she would lose. While some may choose to win at any cost, Rosalie's conscience told her how to reply. Without hesitation, Rosalie replied that she had misspelled the word and had used an *e*. As she walked from the stage, the entire audience stood and applauded her honesty.

We often think that who we *are* determines our actions. More often than not, however, what we *think* determines what we do. And what you think today will determine what you will do and who you will become tomorrow.

Impure Thoughts

To be carnally minded is death; but to be spiritually minded is life and peace.

Romans 8:6 KJV

Let the wicked forsake his way, and the unrighteous man his thoughts; and let him return to the LORD.

Isaiah 55:7 NAS

The word of God is alive and active, sharper than any double-edged sword. It cuts all the way through, to where soul and spirit meet, to where joints and marrow come together. It judges the desires and thoughts of the heart.

Hebrews 4:12 TEV

Let the peace that Christ gives control your thinking, because you were all called together in one body to have peace.

Colossians 3:15 NCV

A Mothballed Conscience

Norman Vincent Peale once stayed home for a month while his wife and children went on vacation. About midway through that month, Peale met a beautiful girl looking for excitement. When she made it clear that she would like to go on a date with Peale, he put his conscience in mothballs and arranged to meet her on Saturday night.

Peale awoke on Saturday morning and decided to take a walk on the beach. He took an old axe along to chop some rope away from the wreck of an old barge that had washed up on the shore. Due to the freshness of the morning and the rhythm of the axe, Peale began to chop in earnest.

As he chopped, a strange thing began to happen. He said, "I felt as if I were outside myself, looking at myself through a kind of fog that was gradually clearing. Suddenly I knew that what I had been planning for that evening was so wrong, so out of keeping with the innermost me." Peale promptly cancelled the date.

Take a good look at the choices you make. Promptly reconsider any that contradict your conscience, and ask God for a clearer view on the right way to proceed.

Jealousy

When you follow your own wrong inclinations your lives will produce these evil results . . . hatred and fighting, jealousy and anger, constant effort to get the best for yourself.

Galatians 5:19-20 TLB

A relaxed attitude lengthens life; jealousy rots it away.

Proverbs 14:30 NLT

Let us behave decently, as in the daytime, not in orgies and drunkenness, not in sexual immorality and debauchery, not in dissension and jealousy.

Romans 13:13

Anger is cruel and destroys like a flood, but no one can put up with jealousy!

Proverbs 27:4 NCV

Be a Bee

Some people let jealousy rule their emotions. They seem to go through their days with their "stingers out," ready to attack others or to defend their positions at the slightest provocation. We should remember, however, the full nature of the "bees" we sometimes seem to emulate.

Bees readily feed each other. The worker bees feed the queen bee, who cannot feed herself. They feed the drones while they work in the hive. They feed their young. Bees will even feed bees from different colonies.

In cold weather, bees cluster together for warmth. They fan their wings to cool the hive in hot weather, thus working for one another's comfort.

When the bees must move to new quarters, scouts report back to the group, performing a dance like the one used to report a find of flowers. When enough scouts have confirmed the suitability of the new location, the bees appear to make a common decision, take wing, and migrate together in what we call a swarm. Their communal caring for each other leaves no room for jealousy.

Only as a last-resort measure of self-defense do bees engage their stingers, but they never use them against their fellow bees. We would do well to learn from them!

Jealousy

Jealousy enrages a man, and he will not spare in the day of vengeance.

Proverbs 6:34 NAS

When the Jewish leaders saw the crowds, they were jealous, and cursed and argued against whatever Paul said.

Acts 13:45 TLB

Jacob's sons became jealous of Joseph and sold him to be a slave in Egypt.

Acts 7:9 NCV

When there is jealousy among you and you quarrel with one another, doesn't this prove that you belong to this world, living by its standards?

1 Corinthians 3:3 TEV

Mining for Gold

Andrew Carnegie, considered to be one of the first to emphasize self-esteem and the potential for inner greatness, was famous for his ability to produce millionaires from among his employees. One day a reporter asked him, "How do you account for the fact you have 43 millionaires working for you?"

Carnegie replied, "They weren't rich when they came. We work with people the same way you mine gold. You have to remove a lot of dirt before you find a small amount of gold."

Andrew Carnegie knew how to bring about change in people. He inspired them to develop their hidden treasure within and then watched with encouragement as their lives became transformed. He responded to their growth with enthusiasm instead of envy.

Many times we respond to others' successes with a negative complaint of "Why them? Why not me?" Envious of someone else's position, status, or abilities, we may even resort to bitter comments about them. Our energies would be better spent reviewing our own lives and looking for the gold hidden inside ourselves. We should follow Andrew Carnegie's example of encouraging others in their successes. If we adopt an attitude of enthusiasm instead of jealousy, everyone will benefit.

Joy

My brethren, count it all joy when you fall into various trials, knowing that the testing of your faith produces patience.

James 1:2-3 NKJV

They that sow in tears shall reap in joy. He that goeth forth and weepeth, bearing precious seed, shall doubtless come again with rejoicing, bringing his sheaves with him.

Psalm 126:5-6 KJV

May the righteous be glad and rejoice before God; may they be happy and joyful.

Psalm 68:3

The kingdom of God is not eating and drinking, but righteousness and peace and joy in the Holy Spirit.

Romans 14:17 NAS

A Joyful Uplook

Legend says that when an architect went to check on the construction of the cathedral of Notre Dame he encountered three different stone masons with identical jobs. He approached the first worker and asked, "What are you doing?"

The man snapped back, "Are you blind? I'm sweating under this blazing sun, cutting these impossible boulders with primitive tools, and putting them together the way I've been told."

The architect quickly backed off, retreated to a second worker, and asked the same question, "What are you doing?" This worker replied matter-of-factly, "I'm shaping these boulders into usable forms, which are then assembled according to plan. It's hard, repetitive work, but I earn five francs a week and that supports my wife and children. It could be worse, could be better."

Feeling somewhat encouraged the architect went on to a third worker, asking, "What are you doing?" The worker lifted his eyes to the sky, smiled, and said, "Why, can't you see? I'm building a beautiful cathedral for God!"

The third workman realized that every job can be done cheerfully. The joy you give to your work or study today will directly impact the satisfaction you feel at the day's end!

Joy

He will yet fill your mouth with laughter and your lips with shouts of joy.

Job 8:21

The redeemed of the LORD shall return, and come with singing unto Zion; and everlasting joy shall be upon their head: they shall obtain gladness and joy; and sorrow and mourning shall flee away.

Isaiah 51:11 KJV

You will show me the path of life; in Your presence is fullness of joy; at Your right hand are pleasures forevermore.

Psalm 16:11 NKJV

Let all who take refuge in Thee be glad, let them ever sing for joy.

Psalm 5:11 NAS

Wholesome Joy

A missionary from Sweden was once urged by his friends to give up his idea of returning to India because it was so hot there. A fellow Swede reminded him, "It's 120 degrees in the shade in that country!" The Swedish missionary jokingly replied, "Vell, ve don't always have to stay in the shade, do ve?"

A joyful outlook is not a sin. It is a God-given escape hatch. Being able to see the lighter side of life is a virtue. And indeed, every vocation and behavior of life has a lighter side, if we are only willing to see it.

A joyful mindset will help us develop a good sense of humor. We will learn to avoid statements that are unsuitable even though they may be funny. We will find that we can laugh at our own mistakes and accept justified criticism graciously and quickly recover from it.

A godly man once concluded his prayer by saying: "Lord, keep me cheerful. Keep me from becoming a cranky old man." Keeping a joyful outlook and developing a good sense of humor will help you avoid becoming a bitter, impatient, critical person. Make wholesome joy a lifetime habit and watch the smiles around you grow!

Knowledge

Praise God forever and ever, because he has wisdom and power. . . . He gives wisdom to those who are wise and knowledge to those who understand.

Daniel 2:20-21 NCV

Wisdom and knowledge will be the stability of your times, and the strength of salvation.

Isaiah 33:6 NKJV

O the depth of the riches both of the wisdom and knowledge of God! how unsearchable are his judgments, and his ways past finding out!

Romans 11:33 KJV

Wisdom will enter your heart, and knowledge will be pleasant to your soul.

Proverbs 2:10 NAS

Know More, Do More

The ability to communicate with the deaf was Alexander Graham Bell's motivation for his life's work. Because his mother and wife were both deaf, Bell felt that if a deaf-mute could talk, he should be able to make metal talk. For five frustrating years, Bell experimented with a variety of materials attempting to make a metal disk that, vibrating in response to sound, could reproduce those sounds and send them over an electrified wire.

During a visit to Washington, D.C., he called on Joseph Henry, a pioneer in electrical research. Bell presented his ideas to him and asked whether he should let someone else perfect the telephone or whether he should do it himself. Henry encouraged Bell to do it himself. When Bell complained that he lacked the necessary knowledge of electricity to find the solution that eluded him, Henry's brief answer was, "Then get it."

So Bell studied electricity. He was so diligent in pursuing an understanding of electrical current that a year later when he obtained a patent for the telephone, patent officials credited Bell with knowing more about electricity than anyone else.

Hard work. Study. Hope. Persistence. These are all "common things." They are the keys, however, to growing in knowledge and to doing things uncommonly well.

Knowledge

A man of understanding and knowledge maintains order.

Proverbs 28:2

The fear of the LORD is the beginning of wisdom, and knowledge of the Holy One is understanding.

Proverbs 9:10

If I have the gift of prophecy and can fathom all mysteries and all knowledge, and if I have a faith that can move mountains, but have not love, I am nothing.

1 Corinthians 13:2

Grow in the grace and knowledge of our Lord and Savior Jesus Christ.

2 Peter 3:18 NAS

Knowing Where to Peck

One day, an intricate piece of equipment on an assembly line broke down. The company's best machinists were called in to diagnose the problem, but they couldn't fix the machine. Finally, they suggested a specialist be brought in. The master mechanic arrived, looked the apparatus over thoroughly, and then asked for the smallest hammer they had on hand. He tapped on a precise area of the machine with the hammer, and said, "Turn on the power. It ought to work now." His small tap with the hammer had apparently released a jammed mechanism. Sure enough, the machine worked.

Later, when the specialist sent a bill for $100, the manager was astounded! It seemed an exorbitant fee for one small tap! The manager asked the specialist to send an itemized statement. He complied, but didn't reduce his fee. The statement read: $1 for pecking; $99 for knowing where to peck.

Learning is a necessary process in life. Doctors must study for years to know how to care for the human body. Automobile mechanics must stay current with the innovative trends in computer diagnostics. Re-certification and retraining is a must for many careers. Put as much learning as you can into every day of your life. You'll have much more to draw upon later!

Laziness

A lazy man sleeps soundly—and he goes hungry!
Proverbs 19:15 TLB

We do not want you to become lazy, but to imitate those who through faith and patience inherit what has been promised.
Hebrews 6:12

Hard work will give you power; being lazy will make you a slave.
Proverbs 12:24 TEV

Warn those who are idle, encourage the timid, help the weak, be patient with everyone.
1 Thessalonians 5:14

Hard-Working Fingerprints

When Joni Eareckson Tada was nominated to serve on the National Council on Disability, she was required to be fingerprinted by the FBI. Though she cooperated as best she could, the agent had a difficult time getting the prints off the pads of her fingers. Finally, after four or five tries, the agent looked at her, shook his head and said, "Lady, I'm sorry, but you just don't have any tread on these fingers of yours."

The agent then turned Joni's hand over so she could get a close look at her own fingers. She discovered that the pads of her fingers were smooth—no ridges showed at all. Joni asked the agent if he had run into this problem before. The agent replied that though he had not personally encountered this situation, he knew that the only folks without fingerprints are those who never use their hands. Of course, in Joni's case, the lack of use was due to her disability. He explained that the ridges on fingers deepen with use. The hands of bricklayers, carpenters, typists, and homemakers who do a lot of dishes always have good prints.

You might think that hard work would wear off good fingerprints. But not so. Hard work enhances them; laziness or any lack of use wears them away. How deep are your fingerprints?

Laziness

The lazy catch no food to cook, but a hard worker will have great wealth.

Proverbs 12:27 NCV

The lazy man longs for many things but his hands refuse to work. He is greedy to get, while the godly love to give!

Proverbs 21:25-26 TLB

You sleep a little; you take a nap. You fold your hands and lie down to rest. Soon you will be as poor as if you had been robbed.

Proverbs 24:33-34 NCV

Respect those who work hard among you.

1 Thessalonians 5:12

Earn Your Pay

Charles Oakley, an NBA all-star, has a reputation for being one of basketball's best rebounders. It's his hard work, however, that has probably contributed the most to his outstanding sports career.

While other professional players seem to have frequent injuries, or are sidelined for other reasons, Oakley hasn't missed a game in three years, even though he has absorbed a great deal of physical punishment and is often pushed, or fouled. He puts in miles and miles each game, running up and down the court. He frequently dives into the stands for loose balls. According to Oakley, his tenacity has an origin: his grandfather Julius Moss.

Moss was a farmer in Alabama who did most of his fieldwork by hand. "Other people had more equipment than he did," Oakley says. "He didn't have a tractor, but he got the work done. No excuses." Moss, who died about five years ago, developed aches and pains in his life, but merely laughed at them and went about his business. Oakley learned a lesson from that—nothing should prevent him from earning a day's pay.

Being focused, dedicated, and disciplined will make the difference between a mediocre life and a great life. Pay your way, and earn your pay.

Loneliness

Turn to me and be gracious to me, for I am lonely and afflicted.

Psalm 25:16 NAS

Even if my father and mother abandon me, the LORD will hold me close.

Psalm 27:10 NLT

"Though the mountains be shaken and the hills be removed, yet my unfailing love for you will not be shaken nor my covenant of peace be removed," says the LORD, who has compassion on you.

Isaiah 54:10

The eternal God is thy refuge, and underneath are the everlasting arms.

Deuteronomy 33:27 KJV

Learning From Isolation

On July 22, 1996, a Japanese teenager set out in a 30-foot yacht on a solo voyage across the Pacific Ocean. On September 13, fourteen-year-old Subaru Takahashi sailed under the Golden Gate Bridge—the youngest person in recorded history to make the 4,600-mile journey alone. Midway into his journey, the motor on his yacht quit. His battery died five days later. Amazingly, Takahashi made the last 2,790 miles of his trip under "sail" power alone.

To prepare for this trip, Takahashi spent five hundred hours of intensive training with yachting experts. Yet this was not his first solo voyage. He began canoeing at age five, and crossed the nineteen-mile Sado Strait in the Sea of Japan in a solo canoe when he was only nine years old.

One of the challenges of a solo sailor's long voyage is the feeling of isolation. Rather than bemoan the loneliness of his venture, Takahashi made solitude his ally, marking the days with a deeper awareness of his abilities and a greater respect for Creation. Solitude ultimately warmed his soul and strengthened his resolve.

Learn to use your time alone as a time for growth. This positive approach will keep you focused and help you achieve your goals too.

Loneliness

Don't be troubled. You trust God, now trust in me.

John 14:1 NLT

He heals the brokenhearted and binds up their wounds.

Psalm 147:3 NKJV

Since we are all one body in Christ, we belong to each other, and each of us needs all the others.

Romans 12:5 NLT

God makes a home for the lonely; He leads out the prisoners into prosperity, only the rebellious dwell in a parched land.

Psalm 68:6 NAS

Overcoming Loneliness

Unaffectionate and uncaring, Mary Lennox had no concept of what life was like outside of India. Largely ignored by her parents and raised by servants, Mary always insisted on having her own way and refused to share her things with other children.

When Mary was nine years old, her parents died of cholera. She was sent to live at her uncle's home in England. The move did nothing to improve her disposition. She still expected everyone to jump at her commands.

Gradually, however, Mary began to change. In her loneliness, Mary asked a robin in the garden to be her friend. She began to treat her maid with more respect, and even began to crave the approval of her maid's little brother, Dickon. Mary began to seek his advice on things and even revealed to him the location of her own little garden. Eventually, Mary convinced her crippled cousin, Colin, to grab hold of life with both hands. By the last page of *The Secret Garden*, Mary's transformation is complete. She is happy with herself and surrounded by friends, and her loneliness is but a distant memory.

To overcome loneliness, you may need a friend. Yet to make a friend, you first must make the choice to be one.

Love

The fruit of the Spirit is love, joy, peace,
longsuffering, gentleness, goodness, faith.
Galatians 5:22 KJV

Above all, love each other deeply, because love
covers over a multitude of sins.
1 Peter 4:8

Whoever loves is a child of God and knows God.
Whoever does not love does not know God, for
God is love.
1 John 4:7-8 TEV

I have loved you with an everlasting love;
therefore I have drawn you with lovingkindness.
Jeremiah 31:3 NAS

Let Them Know

A mother once raised six boys to manhood. As she lay dying, each of her sons came home to see her one final time. Her oldest son knelt quietly by her bedside. Gently wiping her forehead he said to her, "You have always been a good mother to us boys. We love you, Mom."

The weary woman closed her eyes. Giant tears pushed out under the lids and ran down her hollow cheeks. Then she opened her eyes and said to her son, "I prayed that I might be a good mother to you six boys more than I ever prayed for anything else. I was afraid that I should fail in some way. Yet I never knew whether I had failed or not until now. Not one of you ever told me I was a good mother until today. Not one of you ever told me you loved me."

When was the last time you told a parent, grandparent, or other adult how much you appreciate all that he or she has done for you? When was the last time you expressed your love to a brother or sister? Don't delay. The time may come when you no longer have the opportunity.

Love

We need have no fear of someone who loves us perfectly; his perfect love for us eliminates all dread.

1 John 4:18 TLB

Love your enemies, do good, and lend, hoping for nothing in return; and your reward will be great.

Luke 6:35 NKJV

This is my commandment, That ye love one another, as I have loved you.

John 15:12 KJV

Those who do not love their brothers and sisters, whom they have seen, cannot love God, whom they have never seen.

1 John 4:20 NCV

Love Looks Deeper

During high school, Lynn became ill and missed two weeks of school. She returned to school to discover she had nine tests to make up in one week! When she got to the last test, she drew a total blank. She admitted to her teacher, "I don't know any of these answers."

Looking at her paper, the teacher said, "You know the answer to that! You answered a question I asked about that yesterday."

In spite of several hints, Lynn just could not remember. She finally said, "You're just going to have to fail me. I can't remember."

The teacher reached down with his red pencil, and as Lynn watched, he wrote a big, bold A at the top of the page.

"What are you doing?" Lynn asked.

Her teacher replied, "If you had been here and had time to study, that's what you would have earned. So that's what you are going to get."

We should always take into consideration the whole of who a person is, not just their mistakes or blunders. Love looks deeper, beyond what others do to who they are. Love gives others a break once in a while. And that's an amazing gift to give to anyone.

Money/Materialism

The love of money is a root of all kinds of evil, for which some have strayed from the faith in their greediness, and pierced themselves through with many sorrows.

1 Timothy 6:10 NKJV

Give me an eagerness for your decrees; do not inflict me with love for money!

Psalm 119:36 NLT

Wisdom is a shelter as money is a shelter, but the advantage of knowledge is this: that wisdom preserves the life of its possessor.

Ecclesiastes 7:12

Instruct those who are rich in this present world not to be conceited or to fix their hope on the uncertainty of riches, but on God, who richly supplies us with all things to enjoy.

1 Timothy 6:17 NAS

God's Tithe

A church member was having difficulty giving God his tithe. He believed in the concept, and trusted the Bible to be true in other areas of his life, but he still struggled financially. One day he revealed his doubts to his minister, noting that he couldn't see his way clear to give 10 percent of his income to the church when he couldn't even pay his bills.

The pastor listened to the young man's concerns and asked, "If I promise to make up the difference in your bills if you fall short, do you think you could try tithing for just one month?"

The young man thought for a moment and replied, "Sure, if you promise to make up any shortage, I guess I could try tithing for one month."

"Now, what do you think of that," mused the pastor. "You say you'd be willing to put your trust in a man like myself, who possesses so little materially, but you couldn't trust your Heavenly Father who owns the whole universe to do the same!"

The following Sunday, the young man gave his tithe, and continued to do so every Sunday after that. The coins in his pocket were his best reminder: "In God We Trust."

Money/Materialism

Don't store up treasures here on earth where they can erode away or may be stolen. Store them in heaven where they will never lose their value.

Matthew 6:19-20 TLB

Stay away from the love of money; be satisfied with what you have.

Hebrews 13:5 NLT

Be careful and guard against all kinds of greed. Life is not measured by how much one owns.

Luke 12:15 NCV

No one can serve two masters. Either he will hate the one and love the other, or he will be devoted to the one and despise the other. You cannot serve both God and Money.

Matthew 6:24

A Good Investment

The late Spencer Penrose, whose brother was a major political leader in Philadelphia in the late 1800s, was considered the "black sheep" of the family. He chose to live in the West, instead of the East. After graduating from Harvard, Penrose made his way to Colorado in 1891. Not long after his move, Penrose wired his brother and asked for $1,500 so that he could go into a mining venture. His brother telegraphed him $150 instead, warning him against the deal and telling him to use the money to buy a train ticket home.

Years later, Penrose returned to Philadelphia and handed his brother $75,000 in gold coins. It was a return payment, Penrose said, for his brother's "investment" in his mining operation. His brother had qualms about accepting the money, however, and reminded Penrose that he had advised against the venture and had only given him $150.

"That," replied Penrose, "is why I'm giving you only $75,000. If you had sent me the full $1,500 I requested, I would be giving you three-quarters of a million dollars."

Nothing invested; nothing gained. Every harvest requires an initial seed. Be generous in sowing your financial seeds. Plant in good ground and you will receive a good return.

Patience

Be patient and wait for the LORD to act; don't be
worried about those who prosper or those who
succeed in their evil plans.

Psalm 37:7 TEV

It is better to be patient than to be proud. Don't
become angry quickly, because getting angry is
foolish.

Ecclesiastes 7:8-9 NCV

When the Holy Spirit controls our lives he will
produce this kind of fruit in us: love, joy, peace,
patience, kindness, goodness, faithfulness.

Galatians 5:22 TLB

Be completely humble and gentle; be patient,
bearing with one another in love.

Ephesians 4:2

Patience

Twelve-year-old Michael sat on a beach and painstakingly put together a trotline—a maze of ropes to which several fish hooks can be attached. Meanwhile, his parents and two brothers were busy fishing. "You're wasting your time," they called. "Grab a pole and join in the fun."

Undaunted, Michael kept working at his tedious task, even though his family considered it of no value. At dinnertime, when everyone else was ready to call it a day, Michael cast his trotline far into the water, anchoring it to a stick he had plunged deep into the sand. During dinner, his family teased him about coming away from the day's fishing empty-handed. But after dinner, when Michael reeled in his trotline, there were more fish on his line than all of his family had caught put together.

In high school, Michael proved his patient persistence again when he bought his first computer and took it apart to figure out how it worked. Seventeen years later, Michael's patience had taken him from teen to tycoon. Michael Dell became the fourth-largest manufacturer of personal computers in America and the youngest man ever to head a Fortune 500 corporation.

Don't be afraid to start small. Work patiently and persistently. It's where you're headed that counts.

Patience

I waited patiently for the LORD to help me, and he turned to me and heard my cry.

Psalm 40:1 NLT

Let us lay aside every weight, and the sin which doth so easily beset us, and let us run with patience the race that is set before us.

Hebrews 12:1 KJV

Warn those who are unruly, comfort the fainthearted, uphold the weak, be patient with all.

1 Thessalonians 5:14 NKJV

The Lord is not slow about His promise, as some count slowness, but is patient toward you, not wishing for any to perish but for all to come to repentance.

2 Peter 3:9 NAS

Painstaking Patience

We often think of great artists and musicians as having "bursts" of genius. More often, they are models of painstaking patience. Their greatest works tend to have been accomplished over long periods, and often because of extreme hardships. Consider:

Beethoven is said to have rewritten each bar of his compositions at least a dozen times.

Josef Haydn produced more than 800 musical compositions before writing "The Creation," the oratorio for which he is most famous.

Michelangelo's "Last Judgment" is considered one of the twelve master paintings of the ages. It took him eight years to complete and was the result of more than 2,000 sketches and renderings.

Leonardo da Vinci worked on "The Last Supper" for ten years, often working so diligently that he forgot to eat.

When he was quite elderly, the pianist Ignace Paderewski was asked by an admirer, "Is it true that you still practice every day?" Paderewski replied, "Yes, I practice at least six hours a day." The admirer said in awe, "You must have a world of patience." To which Paderewski replied, "I have no more patience than the next fellow. I just use mine."

Are you a model of painstaking patience? Such persistence will pay you great dividends.

Peace

The LORD gives his people strength. The LORD blesses them with peace.

Psalm 29:11 NLT

He will keep in perfect peace all those who trust in him, whose thoughts turn often to the Lord.

Isaiah 26:3 TLB

The peace that Christ gives is to guide you in the decisions you make; for it is to this peace that God has called you together in one body.

Colossians 3:15 TEV

I leave you peace; my peace I give you. I do not give it to you as the world does. So don't let your hearts be troubled or afraid.

John 14:27 NCV

True Peace

Legend says a fisherman caught a fish that was really an enchanted prince. The fisherman let the prince go free, but the fisherman's wife persuaded him to return to the sea and ask the enchanted prince to grant him a wish in return for sparing his life. She told the fisherman to ask that his small hut be turned into a cottage.

The fisherman did as his wife asked. By the time he returned home, the wish was granted. Yet his wife soon tired of the cottage. She sent her husband back to ask for a large, stone castle. Again, this wish was granted.

Alas, his wife tired of this too. The fisherman returned again and again to the enchanted prince, asking for larger and grander things. Yet after each wish was granted, his wife was still unhappy. Finally, the fisherman wished aloud for a peaceful life. Immediately, all of the enchantments disappeared and the fisherman and his wife were back in their old hut.

We waste a lot of energy wishing for things we think will bring us satisfaction. God wants us to savor each moment and recognize his hand in every aspect of our lives. Only then will we find the peace and fulfillment we crave.

Peace

Great peace have they who love [God's] law, and
nothing can make them stumble.

Psalm 119:165

LORD, Thou wilt establish peace for us, since
Thou hast also performed for us all our works.

Isaiah 26:12 NAS

Be perfect, be of good comfort, be of one mind,
live in peace; and the God of love and peace shall
be with you.

2 Corinthians 13:11 KJV

When a man's ways are pleasing to the LORD, he
makes even his enemies to be at peace with him.

Proverbs 16:7 NAS

Tuned for Peace

A Native American visited New York City. As he walked the busy streets with a friend, he suddenly stopped and said, "I hear a cricket."

The friend replied, "It's the noon hour. People are jammed on the sidewalks, cars are honking, the city is full of noise. And you think you can hear a cricket?"

"I'm sure I do," he said. He listened more closely and then walked to the corner of a nearby building. There was a shrub growing in a large cement planter alongside the building. The Indian dug into the leaves underneath the shrub and pulled out a cricket. His friend was astounded.

He then said, "The fact is that my ears are different than yours. It all depends on what your ears have been tuned to hear. Let me show you." At that, he reached into his pocket, pulled out a handful of loose change and dropped the coins on the pavement. Every head within a half block turned toward the noise. "See what I mean?" he said, picking up the coins. "It all depends on what you are listening for."

Listen today to those things that will bring you peace. Heed those things that will prepare you for eternity.

Peer Pressure

We will not be influenced by every new teaching we hear from people who are trying to fool us. They make plans and try any kind of trick to fool people into following the wrong path.

Ephesians 4:14 NCV

I am afraid that someone may fool you with smooth talk. . . . Don't let others spoil your faith and joy with their philosophies, their wrong and shallow answers built on men's thoughts and ideas.

Colossians 2:4,8 TLB

The way of the godly leads to life; their path does not lead to death.

1 Chronicles 26:9 NLT

Jesus said: "I have set an example for you, so that you will do just what I have done for you."

John 13:15 TEV

Go for It

Reverend Stan George decided in 1969 that he was tired of preaching to only nice people. He retired from the pulpit and began to reach out and share the Gospel with bikers and hippies, the kind of people who never went to church. Over the next eighteen years, he motorcycled more than 250,000 miles for the Lord. During that time, he established a national "Christian Motorcyclist Club" that boasted 15,000 members. At age eighty-two, he made a cross-country trip on his trusty motorcycle from San Clemente, California, to Halifax, Nova Scotia.

As George traveled by motorcycle, he used a number of techniques to draw interest to his message. Using magic tricks, jokes, and tales of his odd adventures, George was committed to doing whatever it took so that his listeners would never be bored but would listen to the Gospel.

Is there something you believe God is asking you to do today? Don't let your age, race, or your social standing hold you back. Don't let pressure from your friends, your present career, or your "limitations" stand in your way. Find a method you enjoy that will allow you to pursue your "goal for God." Then, rev up your engine and go for it!

Peer Pressure

Your brother or your son or your daughter or the wife you love or your closest friend may secretly encourage you to worship other gods. . . . But do not let him persuade you; do not even listen to him.

Deuteronomy 13:6,8 TEV

Fully aware of God's death penalty for these crimes . . . they went right ahead and did them anyway, and encouraged others to do them, too.

Romans 1:32 TLB

Each of you should look not only to your own interests, but also to the interests of others. Your attitude should be the same as that of Christ Jesus.

Philippians 2:4-5

In every way be an example of doing good deeds.

Titus 2:7 NCV

Be Yourself

Og Mandino has written: "Every living soul has different talents, different desires, different faculties. Be yourself. Try to be anything else but your genuine self, even if you deceive the entire world, and you will be ten thousand times worse than nothing."

Humans are the only beings who foolishly strive to be something other than who God created them to be. The plants and the animals are content with their lot. Apple trees bear apples. Orange trees bear oranges. Lions roam the earth, while birds soar through the sky. Yet neither one even considers attempting to do what the other was created to do.

Each one of us has been given a calling. That calling is unique. And we have been given special skills and talents that are uniquely ours alone. We must choose to use them, whatever they may be, and forget about someone pressuring us to be something different, to act in a different way, speak different words, live a different lifestyle.

Remember that no one can take your place. So be yourself. For that is the only obligation of all human beings—to be true to you. If you do the very best you can, in the things you do best, then you will know true happiness.

Persecution

Blessed is a man who perseveres under trial; for once he has been approved, he will receive the crown of life, which the Lord has promised to those who love Him.

James 1:12 NAS

Be faithful until death, and I will give you the crown of life.

Revelation 2:10 NKJV

Let us not become weary in doing good, for at the proper time we will reap a harvest if we do not give up.

Galatians 6:9

Watch, stand fast in the faith, be brave, be strong.

1 Corinthians 16:13 NKJV

The Test of Criticism

Former President Harry S. Truman once remarked that no president of our nation has ever escaped abuse or libel from the press. He noted that it was quite common to find a president publicly called a traitor. Truman further concluded that any president who had not fought with Congress or the Supreme Court hadn't done his job correctly.

What is true for an American president is also true for everyone else. No matter how small a person's job may be or no matter how low he may be on a particular organizational chart or strata of society, there will be those who oppose him, ridicule him, and perhaps even challenge him to a fight. That is why no person can expect to conduct himself as if he were trying to win a popularity contest. Rather, a person needs to chart the course he feels compelled to walk in life, and then keep his head held high and his convictions intact.

Every person will eventually face the test of ridicule and criticism as he upholds his principles or defends his morals. Collapsing in the face of persecution will not help. Stand firm in and for your faith, and the Lord will stand with you!

Prayer

When you pray, go away by yourself, all alone, and shut the door behind you and pray to your Father secretly, and your Father, who knows your secrets, will reward you.

Matthew 6:6 TLB

Even before they finish praying to me, I will answer their prayers.

Isaiah 65:24 TEV

Believe that you have received the things you ask for in prayer, and God will give them to you.

Mark 11:24 NCV

The earnest prayer of a righteous person has great power and wonderful results.

James 5:16 NLT

Wade Right Through

A reporter once asked a successful businessman to give him a detailed history of his company. As the man talked at length, the reporter was amazed at the size of the many problems the man had overcome. He finally asked him, "But how did you overcome so many problems of such great magnitude?"

The old gentleman leaned back in his chair, and said, "There's really no trick to it." And then he added, "There are some troubles that seem so high you can't climb over them." The reporter nodded in agreement, thinking of several he was currently facing. "And," the wise businessman went on, "there are some troubles so wide you can't walk around them." Again, the reporter nodded. The man went on, raising his voice dramatically, "And there are some problems so deep you can't dig under them."

Eager for a solution, the reporter said, "Yes, I understand all of that. But what did you do?"

The businessman concluded, "The only way to beat the problem is to pray for strength and guidance; then duck your head and wade right through."

A problem rarely decreases in size while you stand and stare at it. Pray for direction, and follow the guidance you're given.

Prayer

The eyes of the Lord watch over those who do right, and his ears are open to their prayers.

1 Peter 3:12 NLT

When you are praying, if you are angry with someone, forgive him so that your Father in heaven will also forgive your sins.

Mark 11:25 NCV

Call unto me, and I will answer thee, and shew thee great and mighty things, which thou knowest not.

Jeremiah 33:3 KJV

When good people pray, the LORD listens.

Proverbs 15:29 TEV

Unlock the Doors

Early in the twentieth century, Harry Houdini won fame as an escape artist. He claimed he could be put in any jail cell in the country and set himself free within minutes. In town after town, he did just that!

One time, however, something went wrong. Houdini entered a jail cell in his street clothes. The heavy metal doors clanged shut behind him, and he took from his belt a concealed piece of strong but flexible metal. He set to work on the lock to his cell, but something seemed different about this particular lock. For thirty minutes he worked without results. An hour passed. This was long after the time that Houdini normally freed himself. He began to sweat in exasperation. Still, he could not pick the lock.

Finally, feeling failure closing in around him, Houdini cried out in frustration, "God, help me!" He collapsed backward against the jail cell door. To his amazement, the door swung open! It had never been locked in the first place!

How many times are challenges impossible—or doors locked—only because we think they are? When we set our minds and energy on God and ask for His help, we often find that impossible tasks turn into incredible achievements.

Pride

To fear the LORD is to hate evil; I hate pride and
arrogance, evil behavior and perverse speech.

Proverbs 8:13

Everyone who exalts himself will be humbled, and
he who humbles himself will be exalted.

Luke 18:14 NKJV

A man's pride will bring him low, but a humble
spirit will obtain honor.

Proverbs 29:23 NAS

Pride leads to arguments; be humble, take advice
and become wise.

Proverbs 13:10 TLB

Yield Your Pride

While driving down a country road, a man came to a narrow bridge. In front of the bridge was a sign that read, "Yield." Seeing no oncoming cars, the man continued across the bridge and on to his destination. On his way back along this same route, the man came to the same one-lane bridge from the opposite direction. To his surprise, he saw another "Yield" sign posted there.

Curious, he thought. *I'm sure there was a sign posted on the other side.* Sure enough, when he reached the other side of the bridge and looked back, he saw the sign. Yield signs had been placed at both ends of the bridge so that the drivers from both directions would give each other the right of way. It appeared to be a reasonable way to prevent a head-on collision.

If you find yourselves in a combative situation with someone else, don't let your pride keep you from yielding. If they have more authority than you, your lack of submission will put you in a bad position. If you are of equal authority, an exercise of your power will only build resentment in a person better kept as an ally. In either circumstance, the best way to avoid a collision is to yield.

Pride

The patient in spirit is better than the proud in spirit.

Ecclesiastes 7:8 NKJV

Pride will destroy a person; a proud attitude leads to ruin.

Proverbs 16:18 NCV

Do not think of yourself more highly than you should. Instead, be modest in your thinking.

Romans 12:3 TEV

When pride comes, then comes disgrace, but with humility comes wisdom.

Proverbs 11:2

A Truthful Tale

The story is told of an old minister who survived the great Johnstown flood. He loved to tell the story over and over, usually in great detail. Everywhere he went, all he talked about was this great historic event in his life. Eventually, the minister died and went to heaven.

In heaven, he attended a meeting of saints who had gathered to share their life experiences. The minister was very excited. He ran to ask Peter if he might relate the exciting story of his survival from the Johnstown flood.

Peter hesitated for a moment and then said, "Yes, you may share, but just remember that Noah will be in the audience tonight."

When you tell the tales of your life, it is always wise to remember that there may be at least two people hidden somewhere in your audience that will know if what you say is true and accurate or merely prideful boasting. You may have a witness to your words who was there as an eyewitness or someone who has had a similar experience, but on a much greater scale. The best course is always to tell your experience as accurately as possible. Both understatements and exaggerations are prideful lies. Avoid them both.

Priorities

Trust in the LORD with all your heart; do not depend on your own understanding. Seek his will in all you do, and he will direct your paths.

Proverbs 3:5-6 NLT

The LORD has told us what is good. What he requires of us is this: to do what is just, to show constant love, and to live in humble fellowship with our God.

Micah 6:8 TEV

This is what the LORD says: "Stand at the crossroads and look; ask for the ancient paths, ask where the good way is, and walk in it, and you will find rest for your souls."

Jeremiah 6:16

Saul prayed to the LORD, the God of Israel, "Give me the right answer."

1 Samuel 14:41

One to Six

Charles Schwab, one of the first presidents of Bethlehem Steel, once asked an efficiency expert to help him be more productive at work. The efficiency expert told Schwab he could increase Schwab's productivity by at least 50 percent with a simple system. He then handed Schwab a piece of paper and instructed him to write down the six most important tasks he would have to do the next day and number them in the order of their importance.

Then the man said, "Put this paper in your pocket. First thing tomorrow morning, look at the first item and start working on it until it is finished. Then tackle the next item in the same way, and so on. Do this until quitting time every working day. After you've tried this system for a while, have your men try it. Then send me a check for what you think it's worth."

A few weeks later Schwab sent the expert a check for $25,000, calling his advice the most profitable lesson he had ever learned. And in just five years, largely by following this simple system, Bethlehem Steel became the largest independent steel producer in the world.

What are the six most important tasks you have to do tomorrow?

Priorities

The more lowly your service to others, the greater you are. To be the greatest, be a servant.

Matthew 23:11 TLB

Respect the LORD your God, and do what he has told you to do. Love him. Serve the LORD your God with your whole being, and obey the Lord's commands and laws.

Deuteronomy 10:12-13 NCV

Decide today whom you will obey. . . . As for me and my family, we will serve the Lord.

Joshua 24:15 TLB

He will give you all you need from day to day if you live for him and make the Kingdom of God your primary concern.

Matthew 6:33 NLT

Realigned Priorities

Colonel Rahl, the Hessian commander at Trenton, was in the middle of a game of cards when a courier brought a message to him. Rahl casually put the letter in his pocket, but did not read it until the game was finished. When he finally opened the note, he read that Washington was crossing the Delaware River. Rahl quickly rallied his men, but he was too late. He died just before his regiment was taken captive. Because of misplaced priorities, he lost honor, liberty, and his life.

Many a success has been aborted because of misplaced priorities and unexecuted resolutions. In evaluating your immediate future and your ultimate goals, ask yourself these questions:

1. What am I truly doing (or planning to do)? Analyze your own actions and motivations thoroughly.
2. Is this what God requires of me? Given the talents, traits, experiences, and abilities He has given me, does it seem likely that this is what God has prepared for me to do, and desires that I accomplish for His sake?

If your answer to this second question is "no," then your priorities need to be realigned. If your answer is "yes," then do what you know to do with as much energy and enthusiasm as possible!

Protection

You have done so much for those who come to
you for protection.

Psalm 31:19 NLT

When you pass through the waters, I will be with
you; and through the rivers, they will not overflow
you. When you walk through the fire, you will not
be scorched, nor will the flame burn you.

Isaiah 43:2 NAS

The eyes of the LORD run to and fro throughout
the whole earth, to show Himself strong on behalf
of those whose heart is loyal to Him.

2 Chronicles 16:9 NKJV

The Lord is faithful, and he will strengthen and
protect you from the evil one.

2 Thessalonians 3:3

A Kick Start

At a baby giraffe's birth, the newborn is hurled from its mother's body, falls ten feet, and lands on its back. Within seconds, it rolls to an upright position and tucks its legs under its body. The mother giraffe lowers her head long enough to take a quick look at her calf, and then she does what seems to be a very unreasonable thing: she kicks her baby and sends it sprawling head over heels. If it doesn't get up immediately, she kicks it again and again until the calf finally stands up on its wobbly legs.

Yet the mother giraffe isn't finished. She wants her baby to remember how it got up. So, as the newborn stands wobbling beside her, the mother giraffe kicks it off its feet!

In the wild, baby giraffes must be able to get up quickly in order to stay with the herd and avoid becoming a meal for predators. The best way a mother giraffe has of protecting her calf's life is for her to teach it to get up quickly and get moving.

Don't complain if those who love you push you into action. They may be doing you a favor and protecting you from failure!

Protection

He orders his angels to protect you wherever you go.

Psalm 91:11 NLT

The LORD thy God in the midst of thee is mighty; he will save, he will rejoice over thee with joy.

Zephaniah 3:17 KJV

He protects those who are loyal to him, but evil people will be silenced in darkness. Power is not the key to success.

1 Samuel 2:9 NCV

Let all who take refuge in you be glad; let them ever sing for joy. Spread your protection over them, that those who love your name may rejoice in you.

Psalm 5:11

God's Way Is Best

Bruce Larson almost drowned in a storm in the Gulf of Mexico. He was swimming far from shore, trying to reach his drifting boat, when a storm squall overtook him. The waves were seven or eight feet high, and the sky was dark with gale force winds and lightning. His own stupidity and pride had gotten him into the predicament in the first place. His frantic efforts to swim back to shore had only succeeded in weakening him. All he could remember thinking was that he was going to die.

Yet, Larson says, "The Word of the Lord came to me and saved my life. All He said was, 'I'm here, Larson. Can you tread water?' Somehow that action had never occurred to me." Larson followed God's direction until the storm passed, and then he was able to reach the safety of the shore.

Often we get ourselves into hopeless situations and only make matters worse by our frantic efforts to save ourselves. All along God is trying to tell us, "Stand still. Let me take care of you." Is it time for you to pause in your pursuit of a solution to a problem? Give God time to work and to speak His wisdom to you.

Provision

Even lions may get weak and hungry, but those who look to the LORD will have every good thing.
Psalm 34:10 NCV

The LORD will give grace and glory: no good thing will he withhold from them that walk uprightly.

Psalm 84:11 KJV

Indeed, the LORD will give what is good.
Psalm 85:12 NAS

My God shall supply all your need according to His riches in glory by Christ Jesus.
Philippians 4:19 NKJV

Preparing for an Em-Pie-R

Marie Callender made salads in a delicatessen in Los Angeles during World War II. One day her boss asked her to make pies for the lunch crowd. That was the start of a new career for her!

At first Marie baked about ten pies a day at home, dragging hundred-pound flour sacks into her kitchen. Then, in 1948, she and her husband sold their car to buy a Quonset hut, an oven, and a refrigerator for her first commercial kitchen. Two years later, Marie was baking more than two hundred pies a day. Sixteen years later, thousands of pies came out of Marie's ovens each day.

Then Marie and her husband took a daring step. In 1964, they opened their first pie shop in Orange County. They barely broke even that first year, yet her husband and son helped to guide the business to a soaring success. By 1986, Ramada Inns, Inc. bought the family's 115 restaurants for 90 million dollars.

If God could provide a young mother, with a rolling pin and a sack of flour, a new career that would become a baking empire, think what other opportunities await those who will respond to His guidance with hard work and a "better recipe."

Provision

A generous man will prosper; he who refreshes others will himself be refreshed.

Proverbs 11:25

All goes well for the generous man who conducts his business fairly. Such a man will not be overthrown by evil circumstances. God's constant care of him will make a deep impression on all who see it.

Psalm 112:5-6 TLB

Don't be upset, always concerned about what you will eat and drink. (For the pagans of this world are always concerned about all these things.) Your Father knows that you need these things.

Luke 12:29-30 TEV

God can give you more blessings than you need. Then you will always have plenty of everything.

2 Corinthians 9:8 NCV

Use What You Have for Others

He received a medical degree from New York University College of Medicine and an appointment to the Virus Research Laboratory at the University of Pittsburgh. He has been given the Presidential Medal of Freedom. And the U.S. Army asked him to develop a vaccine against influenza.

Yet Jonas Salk used the many opportunities he was given to find a way to help others. He is best known for his contribution to the fight against polio. He and his team of researchers diligently worked to prepare a neutralized polio virus that would serve as an immunizing agent against polio. By 1952, they had created a vaccine and in 1955, the vaccine was released for widespread use in the United States, virtually ending the ravaging effects of the disease.

God may provide you with many opportunities in your life. What will ultimately count, however, is what you do with what you have received and the skills and traits you have developed. Find a way to give, create, or generate something today that will benefit others. Use what God has provided to enrich someone else. You will find in such an attitude not only a potential for fame and reward, but also great personal satisfaction and God's bountiful provision.

Reading the Bible

The whole Bible was given to us by inspiration from God and is useful to teach us what is true and to make us realize what is wrong in our lives.

2 Timothy 3:16 TLB

The word of God is alive and active, sharper than any double-edged sword. It cuts all the way through, to where soul and spirit meet. . . . It judges the desires and thoughts of man's heart.

Hebrews 4:12 TEV

Your word is a lamp to my feet and a light to my path.

Psalm 119:105 NKJV

Do not let this Book of the Law depart from your mouth; meditate on it day and night, so that you may be careful to do everything written in it. Then you will be prosperous and successful.

Joshua 1:8

Rooted in God

Psalm 1 describes two ways to view and experience life. One approach is scornful, negative, pessimistic, and cynical. The psalmist says those who live this way have shallow roots and will wither when a dry season comes because they have no true source of nourishment in their lives.

The other approach to life accepts the things of God and results in a life that is happy, principled, well grounded, and delightful. The person who follows this way is likened to a tree planted near a steadily flowing stream. His roots go deep and are always supplied with life-giving water even in times of trouble or drought.

The Bible clearly says that those who leave God out of their lives will not have staying power. Nothing will truly satisfy them. Nothing will seem worthwhile. Yet those who embrace God and the things of God will produce, multiply, and create things of lasting value for themselves and others.

Evaluate your life today. Are you satisfied with its direction? How deep are your roots in God's soil? Are you planted beside His life-giving stream? If you wish to find true satisfaction, let the Bible's words shape your lifestyle.

Reading the Bible

So shall My word be that goes forth from My mouth; it shall not return to Me void, but it shall accomplish what I please, and it shall prosper in the thing for which I sent it.

Isaiah 55:11 NKJV

Study to shew thyself approved unto God, a workman that needeth not to be ashamed, rightly dividing the word of truth.

2 Timothy 2:15 KJV

I have not neglected your instructions, because you yourself are my teacher.

Psalm 119:102 TEV

The teachings of the LORD are perfect; they give new strength. The rules of the LORD can be trusted; they make plain people wise.

Psalm 19:7 NCV

A Lasting Legacy

Abraham Lincoln is often heralded as the greatest American president. His spirituality was undoubtedly the greatest reason for the decisions that led to his success, and he repeatedly referred to his indebtedness to and regard for the Bible.

Lincoln began reading the Bible in his boyhood. Its influence upon him increased over the years. Whenever he addressed the public, he quoted from the Bible more than from any other book. Lincoln's literary style mirrored the style of the Bible, especially the writings of the prophets of Israel. His deeply moving second inaugural speech is strongly reminiscent of the book of Isaiah. Lincoln also thought in terms of biblical ideas and convictions to an extent that has been unparalleled among modern statesmen.

Moreover, Lincoln was a man of prayer. Without apology or self-consciousness, Lincoln did not hesitate to request the prayers of others or to acknowledge that he himself prayed often. He regarded prayer as a necessity and routinely spoke of seeking divine guidance as though it was an entirely natural and reasonable thing to do.

Never curtail your pursuit of God. Never stop reading God's Word. It is the most important thing you can do to leave a lasting legacy of accomplishment and purpose.

Rejection

Jesus said: "Those the Father has given me will come to me, and I will never reject them."
John 6:37 NLT

Those who know you, LORD, will trust you; you do not abandon anyone who comes to you.
Psalm 9:10 TEV

The Lord will not forsake his people, for they are his prize.
Psalm 94:14 TLB

He who rejects this instruction does not reject man but God, who gives you his Holy Spirit.
1 Thessalonians 4:8

Choose Hope

In her early struggle to launch a theater career, Carol Burnett was called to audition for a revival of Rodgers and Hart's *Babes in Arms*. She felt her dreams were about to come true. Yet when her audition came, Carol did not do well, and she did not get the part.

Carol returned to her apartment where her sister Chrissy was hoping to hear good news. Carol told her sister what had happened and burst into tears because of the director's rejection. Chrissy gave her a hug and cheered her up by reminding her that when one door closes, another one will often open. By dinnertime, Chrissy had given her so much hope that Carol was laughing when the phone rang. It was a call for another audition—this time for the lead in *Once Upon a Mattress*. Carol got the lead role she had always dreamed of, worked for a legendary director, and watched her career begin to grow.

Thornton Wilder once said, "In response to hope the imagination is aroused to picture every possible issue, to try every door, to fit together even the most heterogeneous pieces in the puzzle." Despite the rejection you may experience, choose to be hopeful today. It is the best self-motivator possible.

Rejection

You have been my helper. Do not reject me or forsake me, O God my Savior. Though my father and mother forsake me, the LORD will receive me.

Psalm 27:9-10

The LORD will not forsake His people, for His great name's sake, because it has pleased the LORD to make you His people.

1 Samuel 12:22 NKJV

God will not reject a man of integrity, nor will He support the evildoers.

Job 8:20 NAS

The LORD your God goes with you; he will never leave you nor forsake you.

Deuteronomy 31:6

Labor On

In 1894, Guglielmo retreated to his room on the third floor. All during vacation he had read books and filled notebooks with squiggly diagrams. Now, the time had come to get to work.

Every day, he rose early, working all day and long into the night, to the point that his mother became alarmed. He had never been a robust person, but now he was appallingly thin. His face was drawn, and his eyes were often glazed with fatigue. Finally, the day came when he announced that his experiment was ready. He invited the family to his room and, by pushing a button, he succeeded in ringing a bell on the first floor! While his mother was amazed, his father was not. He saw no use in sending a signal so short a distance.

Guglielmo Marconi accepted his father's words of rejection and labored on. Little by little, he made changes in his wireless telegraph so that he could send a signal from one house to the next, then one hill to the next, and then beyond the hill. His forerunner of the radio was perfected partly by inspiration, but mostly by perseverance.

When inspiration and perseverance meet rejection head-on, the result can only be achievement.

Relationships

Get along with each other, and forgive each other. If someone does wrong to you, forgive that person because the Lord forgave you.

Colossians 3:13 NCV

Don't quarrel with anyone. Be at peace with everyone, just as much as possible.

Romans 12:18 TLB

Help carry one another's burdens, and in this way you will obey the law of Christ.

Galatians 6:2 TEV

Be kind to each other, tenderhearted, forgiving one another, just as God through Christ has forgiven you.

Ephesians 4:32 NLT

Reach Out and Build

Helen Keller suffered a fever as a baby that left her deaf and blind. She overcame the difficult physical challenge of living with these handicaps and learned to read and write Braille. Her life inspired millions, and she was invited to visit every president in the White House from her childhood on.

What many people don't know, however, is how hard Helen worked as an adult to foster good relationships between sighted people and the blind. After graduating from Radcliffe College, Helen worked to help others until her death at the age of eighty-eight. She wrote numerous articles. She gave lectures and helped raise more than two million dollars for the American Foundation for the Blind. On her eightieth birthday, the American Foundation for Overseas Blind honored her by establishing the Helen Keller International Award for those who give outstanding help to the blind.

Not only are each of us called to overcome our own faults and limitations, but we are also asked to help build strong relationships with others. We are to use our talents for God's purposes, putting all our minds, hearts, and energies to the work He sets before us, strengthening relationships and building new ones as He gives us opportunity.

Relationships

Do not be bound together with unbelievers; for what partnership have righteousness and lawlessness, or what fellowship has light with darkness?

2 Corinthians 6:14 NAS

As iron sharpens iron, so a man sharpens the countenance of his friend.

Proverbs 27:17 NKJV

Love one another deeply, from the heart.

1 Peter 1:22

Give everyone what you owe him: If you owe taxes, pay taxes; if revenue, then revenue; if respect, then respect; if honor, then honor. Let no debt remain outstanding, except the continuing debt to love one another.

Romans 13:7-8

Lifelong Friends

Mr. Young got his start in farming on a rented farm in Iowa. In need of financial backing to expand his operation, he turned to Art Swasand at the bank. Art did business the old-fashioned way: a client's character was an important part of the deal.

Art had a reputation for going the extra mile and doing whatever it took to develop and maintain successful working relationships. When Mr. Young's tractor broke down, Art drove out to visit him. Once he understood what was needed to get the tractor running again, Art financed the parts on the spot.

Over the years the two men financed and paid off farm machinery, set up financial plans, purchased land, and raised their families. Each man became successful and did what they loved best, with integrity but without fanfare. Because of their close working relationship Mr. Young said, "In more ways than one Art was a father, a brother, a confidant, a friend. He was my ideal of a man."

Those around you will see the way you treat your friends and acquaintances. If you live a life of upright values and strong faith, you will not only chart a straight path through life, you will also build cherished, lifelong relationships.

Self-control

Those who belong to Christ Jesus have nailed the passions and desires of their sinful nature to his cross.

Galatians 5:24 NLT

How can a young person live a pure life? By obeying your word.

Psalm 119:9 NCV

Set a watch, O LORD, before my mouth; keep the door of my lips. Incline not my heart to any evil thing.

Psalm 141:3-4 KJV

I urge you therefore, brethren, by the mercies of God, to present your bodies a living and holy sacrifice, acceptable to God, which is your spiritual service of worship.

Romans 12:1 NAS

Take It in Stride

Astronaut Shannon Lucid was not supposed to set an American record for time spent in space. However, her assignment was extended because of technical difficulties with shuttle booster rockets and adverse weather conditions. Lucid ultimately stayed in space 188 days, setting a U.S. space endurance record and a world record for a female astronaut.

What many reports failed to note in the wake of Lucid's record-setting stay on the Russian space station *Mir* was the excellent reputation that Lucid had with her Russian hosts. Lucid's reputation was based not only on her technical expertise as an astronaut, but also on the fact that her Russian counterparts never once heard her complain during her six-month stay. Every time Lucid was notified of a shuttle delay, she took the news in stride.

Valery Ryumin, a Russian space manager, noted that Lucid reacted like Russian cosmonauts do when their missions are extended. Ryumin said that Russia deliberately chooses cosmonauts "who are strong enough not to show any feelings" when they receive bad news.

Complaining not only makes you feel negative, but it spreads your negativity to others. Even an unpleasant or disappointing situation can become positive when you exercise self-control, maintain a good attitude, and speak uplifting words.

Self-control

Do not let any unwholesome talk come out of your mouths, but only what is helpful for building others up according to their needs, that it may benefit those who listen.

Ephesians 4:29

Follow the Lord's rules for doing his work, just as an athlete either follows the rules or is disqualified and wins no prize.

2 Timothy 2:5 TLB

Knowing God leads to self-control. Self-control leads to patient endurance, and patient endurance leads to godliness.

2 Peter 1:6 NLT

Clothe yourselves with the Lord Jesus Christ, and do not think about how to gratify the desires of the sinful nature.

Romans 13:14

Keep Your Shirt On

In the 1950s, President Truman appointed Newbold Morris to investigate allegations of crime and mismanagement in high levels of government. A few months later, Morris was himself in the witness chair in the Senate hearing room, answering a barrage of questions from a subcommittee about the sale of some ships by his New York company.

The investigation was intense. The subcommittee's questions were becoming increasingly accusatory. Morris's face first recorded pain, then surprise, and finally anger. Amidst a flurry of irate murmurs in the room, he rose, reached into his coat, and produced a sheet of white paper. Then he shouted: "Wait a minute. I have a note here from my wife. It says, 'Keep your shirt on!'"

Everyone in the room burst into laughter, temporarily diffusing the angry situation.

Anger that is allowed to rage on eventually plays out in one of two ways: abuse or estrangement. Abuse—both physical blows and emotional wounding—and estrangement are painful situations. Reconciliation can be very difficult, and the healing process is often a long one. How much better it is to control yourself and your anger. Channel the intense feelings of rage into positive, productive expenditures of energy, and whenever possible, lighten the moment.

Self-discipline

Do not give in to bodily passions, which are always at war against the soul.

1 Peter 2:11 TEV

Everything in the world—the cravings of sinful man, the lust of his eyes and the boasting of what he has and does—comes not from the Father but from the world.

1 John 2:16

Let my heart be blameless regarding Your statutes, that I may not be ashamed.

Psalm 119:80 NKJV

Those who belong to Christ Jesus have crucified their own sinful selves. They have given up their old selfish feelings and the evil things they wanted to do.

Galatians 5:24 NCV

Give Yourself a Check-Up

A young boy walked into a drugstore one day and asked to use the telephone. He dialed a number and said, "Hello, Dr. Anderson, do you want to hire a boy to cut your grass and run errands for you?" After a pause he said, "Oh, you already have a boy? Are you completely satisfied with the job he's doing?" Another pause. "All right then, good-bye, Doctor."

As the boy thanked the druggist and prepared to leave, the druggist called to him. "Just a minute, son. I couldn't help but overhear your conversation. If you are looking for work, I could use a boy like you."

"Thank you, sir," the boy replied, "but I already have a job."

"You do?" the druggist responded. "But didn't you just try to get a job from Dr. Anderson?"

"No, sir," the boy said. "I already work for Dr. Anderson. I was just checking up on myself."

A self-disciplined individual looks for ways to improve performance and avoid mistakes. Ask those with whom and for whom you work to give you suggestions on how you might do better, achieve more, and grow to the next level. When you check up on yourself, others won't feel it necessary to do so!

Self-discipline

God did not give us a spirit of timidity, but a spirit of power, of love and of self-discipline.

2 Timothy 1:7

I advise you to obey only the Holy Spirit's instructions. He will tell you where to go and what to do, and then you won't always be doing the wrong things your evil nature wants you to.

Galatians 5:16 TLB

Control yourselves and be careful! The devil, your enemy, goes around like a roaring lion looking for someone to eat. Refuse to give in to him, by standing strong in your faith.

1 Peter 5:8-9 NCV

Let the Lord Jesus Christ take control of you, and don't think of ways to indulge your evil desires.

Romans 13:14 NLT

You Can Fly

Michael Stone had always dreamed of flying. A young man of extreme dedication and discipline, Michael chose to pursue the "flying" of pole vaulting. At age fourteen, he began a regimented program to achieve his goal. He worked out every other day with weights, and on alternate days, he ran. Michael's father, his coach and trainer, monitored the program. Besides being an athlete, Michael was also an honor-roll student and helped his parents with their farm.

At age seventeen, Michael faced his greatest athletic challenge. People watched as the pole was set at 17 feet—several inches higher than Michael's personal best. He cleared it, and then cleared the pole again at 17 feet 2 inches and again at 17 feet 4 inches.

In his final vault, Michael needed to fly 9 inches higher than he ever had. Taking deep breaths to relax, he sprinted down the runway to an effortless takeoff. Michael began to fly and cleared the bar, setting a new National and International Junior Olympics record. His years of practice and self-discipline in pursuit of a goal had resulted in victory, one made even sweeter by the fact that Michael Stone is blind.

Choose to endure today in the pursuit of your goals; with self-discipline, they are within reach!

Self-pity

Let not your heart be troubled; you believe in God, believe also in Me.

John 14:1 NKJV

God has made us what we are. In Christ Jesus, God made us to do good works, which God planned in advance for us to live our lives doing.

Ephesians 2:10 NCV

We are afflicted in every way, but not crushed; perplexed, but not despairing; persecuted, but not forsaken; struck down, but not destroyed.

2 Corinthians 4:8-9 NAS

We say with confidence, "The Lord is my helper; I will not be afraid. What can man do to me?"

Hebrews 13:6

Don't Despair

While in the midst of contending with the geographic problems of building the Panama Canal, Colonel George Washington Goethals had to endure a great deal of criticism from those back home who predicted he would never complete his great task. The visionary builder continued on, refusing to give in to their doomsday attitudes or to succumb to self-pity because of their carping.

"Aren't you going to answer your critics?" a reporter asked him.

"In time I will," Goethals replied.

"How? And when?" the reporter inquired.

The colonel merely smiled and said simply, "I'll answer my detractors with a finished canal."

In the same way Ole Bull, a violinist in the nineteenth century, was once offered space in the New York Herald to answer his critics. He said, "I think it is best that they write against me. I shall play against them."

The finest response to one's detractors is faithfully doing the very best one can do—consistently, persistently, and insistently. Diligent performance disarms criticism and debilitates self-pity. It wastes no time and suffers no loss. Make your steady, faithful work your best defense. It will not only prove your critics wrong, but also strengthen your resolve and build your self-esteem.

Self-pity

Those who wait on the LORD shall renew their
strength; they shall mount up with wings like
eagles, they shall run and not be weary, they shall
walk and not faint.

Isaiah 40:31 NKJV

Peace I leave with you, my peace I give unto you:
not as the world giveth, give I unto you. Let not
your heart be troubled, neither let it be afraid.

John 14:27 KJV

I will give them a crown to replace their ashes,
and the oil of gladness to replace their sorrow, and
clothes of praise to replace their spirit of sadness.

Isaiah 61:3 NCV

I have learned, in whatsoever state I am, therewith
to be content.

Philippians 4:11 KJV

Different Outlook, Different Outcome

Kevin was a high school football star and later, an avid wrestler, boxer, hunter, and skin-diver. Then tragically, a broken neck left him paralyzed from the chest down. His doctors were hopeful that one day, with therapy, he would be able to walk with the help of braces and crutches.

The former athlete could not reconcile himself to his physical limitations, however, so he prevailed upon two of his friends to leave him alone in a wooded area. After they left, he held a twelve-gauge shotgun to his abdomen and pulled the trigger, committing suicide at the age of twenty-four.

At the age of nineteen, Jim was stabbed, leaving him paralyzed from the middle of his chest down. Although confined to a wheelchair, he lives alone, cooks his own meals, washes his clothes, and cleans his house. He drives himself in a specially equipped automobile. He has written three books, and was the photographer for the first book on the history of wheelchair sports. Thirty years after his injury, he made a successful parachute jump, landing precisely on his target.

Kevin and Jim had nearly identical injuries and physical limitations. Their outlook, however, led to vastly different outcomes. What is your outlook on life today?

Sexual Pressure

A prostitute is as dangerous as a deep pit, and an unfaithful wife is like a narrow well. They ambush you like robbers and cause many men to be unfaithful to their wives.

Proverbs 23:27-28 NCV

The lips of an immoral woman drip honey, and her mouth is smoother than oil; but in the end she is bitter as wormwood, sharp as a two-edged sword.

Proverbs 5:3-4 NKJV

[Folly] says to those who lack judgment: "Stolen water is sweet; food eaten in secret is delicious!" But little do they know that the dead are there, that her guests are in the depths of the grave.

Proverbs 9:16-18

Run from sex sin. No other sin affects the body as this one does. When you sin this sin it is against your own body.

1 Corinthians 6:18 TLB

Heed His Advice

A group of explorers set out in search of the North Pole. One of the team members was a Swede named Dr. Solander. One day, while some distance from their camp, a cold south wind and driving snow caught the party of explorers by surprise.

Dr. Solander gathered the men around him and gravely said, "I have had some experience of this in my own country. Now, heed my advice, for upon it depends your lives. We must resolutely set our faces to get back to camp, and with never a stop, for the danger lies in falling asleep. I warn you, that as your blood grows cold, you will ask to be allowed to rest. Do not permit it for a moment. Remember that the wish to stop is the first symptom of the blood refusing to circulate. To yield to it is death."

The party moved on, and kept moving until all arrived safely at the camp. No one tried to stop. All had heard, and heeded, Dr. Solander's warning.

God warns about the perils of sexual promiscuity and promises that yielding to such temptations will only lead to pain. May we heed God's warnings with as much determination as the explorers heeded Dr. Solander's.

Sexual Pressure

Each of you should learn to control his own body in a way that is holy and honorable, not in passionate lust like the heathen, who do not know God.

1 Thessalonians 4:4-5

Our bodies were not made for sexual immorality. They were made for the LORD, and the LORD cares about our bodies.

1 Corinthians 6:13 NLT

Since you are God's people, it is not right that any matters of sexual immorality or indecency or greed should even be mentioned among you.

Ephesians 5:3 TEV

God did not call us to be impure, but to live a holy life.

1 Thessalonians 4:7

Promiscuity Produces Pain

The 1960s were known for many rebellions, among them the sexual revolution. "Free love" spilled over from the hippie movement into the mainstream of American culture. Premarital sexual experiences sanctioned by the "new morality" were openly flaunted. Extra-marital affairs were excused. Multiple sex partners became an accepted norm in hippie communes.

One of the unexpected results of this trend, however, received little publicity. Dr. Francis Braceland, past president of the American Psychiatric Association and editor of the *American Journal of Psychiatry*, reports that an increasing number of young people were admitted to mental hospitals during this time! In discussing this finding at a National Methodist Convocation on Medicine and Theology, Braceland concluded, "a more lenient attitude about premarital sex imposed stresses on some college women that were severe enough to cause emotional breakdown."

Looking back over the years since the "new morality" has been accepted by a high percentage of Americans, one finds a rising number of rapes, abortions, divorces, premarital pregnancies, and single-family homes. Cases of sexually transmitted diseases, including herpes and HIV, have more than tripled in some areas because of relaxed moral standards. The evidence is compelling: the old morality produced safer, healthier, and happier people! God's way is always best.

Spiritual Growth

Put on all of God's armor so that you will be able to stand firm against all strategies and tricks of the Devil.

Ephesians 6:11 NLT

Grow in grace, and in the knowledge of our Lord and Savior Jesus Christ. To him be glory both now and for ever. Amen.

2 Peter 3:18 KJV

The righteous man will flourish like the palm tree, he will grow like a cedar in Lebanon.

Psalm 92:12 NAS

This is my prayer: that your love may abound more and more in knowledge and depth of insight, so that you may be able to discern what is best and may be pure and blameless until the day of Christ.

Philippians 1:9-10

Give Up and Grow

In *The Great Divorce*, C.S. Lewis tells the story of a ghost who carries a little red lizard on his shoulder. The lizard constantly twitches its tail and whispers to the ghost, who all the while urges him to be quiet. When a bright and shining presence appears and offers to rid the ghost of his troublesome "baggage," the ghost refuses. He realizes that to quiet the lizard, it would be necessary to kill it.

The ghost begins to reason with the shining presence. Perhaps the lizard need not die but instead might be trained, suppressed, put to sleep, or removed "gradually." The shining presence responds that the only recourse is death.

Finally, the ghost gives permission for the presence to twist the lizard away from him. As the presence flings the lizard to the ground, its back is broken. In that moment, the ghost becomes a real man, and the lizard becomes a beautiful stallion. The man leaps onto the great horse and rides off into the sunrise.

When you give God your all, you put yourself in a position to receive His all. Give up your "lizard," that thing that keeps you chained to sin, and grow strong in your faith.

Stability

He will not fear evil tidings; his heart is steadfast, trusting in the LORD.

Psalm 112:7 NAS

Grass withers and flowers fade, but the word of our God endures forever.

Isaiah 40:8 TEV

He who doubts is like a wave of the sea, blown and tossed by the wind. . . . He is a double-minded man, unstable in all he does.

James 1:6,8

When there is moral rot within a nation, its government topples easily; but with honest, sensible leaders there is stability.

Proverbs 28:2 TLB

A Promise Kept

Stephen Covey once counseled a man who had a reputation for procrastination and selfishness. The man could rarely be counted on to keep his commitments. Covey challenged him to a simple change. "Will you get up in the morning when you say you're planning to get up?" Covey asked. "Will you just get up in the morning?"

The man saw little point in what Covey was challenging him to do, but when Covey asked him to commit to getting up at a certain time for a week, the man agreed to do so.

Covey saw the man a week later and asked, "Did you do it?" The man replied in the affirmative, so Covey then asked, "What's the next thing you're going to commit to do?"

Little by little, the man began to make and keep commitments. No one knew of the plan but Covey and one friend. Over time, the man made remarkable changes. His relationships improved, his promises were kept, and his integrity was regained. His entire life stabilized because he began to keep his promises—first to himself and then to others. When you keep your word to yourself, it becomes easier to keep your word to others and produces tremendous peace of mind and stability in your life.

Stability

By justice a king gives a country stability, but one who is greedy for bribes tears it down.

Proverbs 29:4

Wisdom and knowledge will be the stability of your times, and the strength of salvation; the fear of the LORD is His treasure.

Isaiah 33:6 NKJV

The eye is a light for the body. If your eyes are good, your whole body will be full of light. But if your eyes are evil, your whole body will be full of darkness.

Matthew 6:22-23 NCV

Be steadfast, immovable, always abounding in the work of the Lord, knowing that your labor is not in vain in the Lord.

1 Corinthians 15:58 NKJV

Small Bits Matter a Lot

Have you ever watched an icicle form on a cold winter day? Did you notice how the dripping water froze, one drop at a time, until the icicle was a foot long, or more? If the water was clean, the icicle remained clear and sparkled brightly in the sun; but if the water was slightly muddy, the icicle looked cloudy, its beauty spoiled.

In just this manner our character is formed. Each thought or feeling adds its influence. Each decision we make, whether about matters great or small, will contribute to our singular identity. Every bit that we take into our minds and souls—be they impressions, experiences, visual images, or the words of others—will help to create our character.

We must remain concerned at all times about the "droplets" that influence our lives. In large part these small bits of experience shape the stability or instability of our lives. Habits of hate, falsehood, and evil intent will mar us like the muddied icicle, eventually destroying us. But acts that develop habits of love, truth, and goodness silently mold and fashion us into the image of God and give us a firm foundation, building our character like the crystal clear icicle.

Strength

The LORD is my rock, and my fortress, and my deliverer; my God, my strength, in whom I will trust; my buckler, and the horn of my salvation, and my high tower.

Psalm 18:2 KJV

He gives strength to those who are tired and more power to those who are weak.

Isaiah 40:29 NCV

My soul melts from heaviness; strengthen me according to Your word.

Psalm 119:28 NKJV

I have the strength to face all conditions by the power that Christ gives me.

Philippians 4:13 TEV

See the Stars

During the darkest days of the Civil War, the hopes of the Union Army nearly died. When certain goals seemed unreachable, the army's leaders turned to President Abraham Lincoln for solace, guidance, and a renewal of hope. A delegation called at the White House and detailed a long list of crises facing the nation. Lincoln replied with this story:

"Years ago a young friend and I were out one night when a shower of meteors fell from the clear November sky. The young man was frightened, but I told him to look up into the sky, past the shooting stars, to the fixed stars beyond, shining serene in the firmament. I said, 'Let us not mind the meteors, but let us keep our eyes on the stars.'"

When times are troubled or life seems to be changing greatly, keep your inner eyes of faith and hope fixed on those things you know are lasting and sure. Don't limit your gaze to what you know or who you know, but focus on Whom you know. God alone—and a relationship with Him Who is eternal—is the supreme goal. God never changes, and His strength is always available to you.

Strength

In returning and rest shall ye be saved; in quietness and in confidence shall be your strength.

Isaiah 30:15 KJV

I pray that out of his glorious riches he may strengthen you with power through his Spirit in your inner being, so that Christ may dwell in your hearts through faith.

Ephesians 3:16-17

They that wait upon the Lord shall renew their strength. They shall mount up with wings like eagles; they shall run and not be weary; they shall walk and not faint.

Isaiah 40:31 TLB

The LORD is my light and my salvation; whom shall I fear? the LORD is the strength of my life; of whom shall I be afraid?

Psalm 27:1 KJV

Strong Roots

Consider these facts about trees and roots:
- Forestry experts estimate that the root spread of many trees is equal to the spread of their branches.
- As much as one-tenth of a tree is concealed in its roots.
- The combined length of the roots of a large oak tree would total several hundred miles.
- Hair-like as some tree roots are, an entire system of them can still exert tremendous pressure, uprooting boulders that weigh many tons.
- A tree's root system serves two functions: to anchor the tree, and to collect moisture, without which the tree could not thrive.
- In Herbstein, Germany, town officials require every newly married couple to plant three birch saplings along their "Marriage Road."
- A tree's roots adapt to strengthen it against whatever may try to attack it. If it is wind, the roots grow thick and deep. If it is drought, the roots grow toward water.

People have "roots" too, and our roots have a direct effect on our branches and our fruit. Our roots are established in the inward matters of life, our thoughts and motives, which enable us to produce strength on the outside. Are you building strong roots?

Stress

In my distress I cried out to the LORD . . . He heard me from his sanctuary; my cry reached his ears.

2 Samuel 22:7 NLT

Jesus said, "Don't let your hearts be troubled. Trust in God, and trust in me."

John 14:1 NCV

Leave your troubles with the LORD, and he will defend you; he never lets honest men be defeated.

Psalm 55:22 TEV

Fear not, for I am with you. Do not be dismayed. I am your God. I will strengthen you; I will help you; I will uphold you with my victorious right hand.

Isaiah 41:10 TLB

The Right Results

Sadie Delaney's father taught her to try to do better than her competition. Shortly before she received her teaching license, a supervisor came to watch her and two other student teachers. Their assignment was to teach a class to bake cookies. Since the supervisor didn't have time for each student teacher to go through the entire lesson, she assigned a portion of the lesson to each of the student teachers. Sadie was assigned to teach the girls how to serve and clean up.

The first student teacher panicked, forgot to halve the recipe, or preheat the oven. The second girl was so behind because of the first girl's errors that the students made a mess in forming and baking the cookies.

Then it was Sadie's turn. She said to the girls, "We'll have to work together as a team." They quickly baked the remaining dough. Several girls scrubbed pans as soon as the cookies came out of the oven. Within ten minutes, they had several dozen perfect cookies and a clean kitchen. The supervisor was so impressed she offered Sadie a substitute teacher's license on the spot.

Do what it takes to get right results. Your life will be marked with less stress and more success!

Stress

In the day of my trouble I will call upon You, for You will answer me.

Psalm 86:7 NKJV

Let us not become weary in doing good, for at the proper time we will reap a harvest if we do not give up.

Galatians 6:9

Consider it all joy, my brethren, when you encounter various trials, knowing that the testing of your faith produces endurance.

James 1:2-3 NAS

Come to me, all of you who are weary and carry heavy burdens, and I will give you rest.

Matthew 11:28 NLT

An Unraveled Witness

A minister was scheduled to speak at an all-day conference. He failed to set his alarm, however, and he overslept. In his haste to make up for lost time, he cut himself while shaving. When he went to iron his wrinkled shirt, he scorched it because the iron was too hot. To make matters worse, he noticed that he had a flat tire on his car.

By the time the minister finished changing the tire he was an hour behind schedule. He figured that if he hurried, he might be only a few minutes late for the first session. He raced through town, only to be stopped by a policeman for speeding.

The agitated minister said sharply, "Officer, go ahead and give me a ticket. Everything else has gone wrong today."

The policeman quietly responded, "I used to have stressful days like yours before I became a Christian."

The minister hung his head in shame. He had forgotten to start his day with God and had allowed stress to unravel his Christian witness.

Your Christian witness shows far more in your everyday lifestyle than in what you have to say about your Christianity. Start your day with prayer and don't let stress undo your witness.

Swearing

Keep your tongue from evil and your lips from speaking lies.

Psalm 34:13

Let no corrupt word proceed out of your mouth, but what is good for necessary edification, that it may impart grace to the hearers.

Ephesians 4:29 NKJV

I tell you this, that you must give account on judgment day of every idle word you speak.

Matthew 12:36 NLT

I will watch my ways and keep my tongue from sin; I will put a muzzle on my mouth.

Psalm 39:1

Your Calling Card

The oldest sister of Daniel Webster married a man named John Colby, the most wicked, godless man in his neighborhood when it came to swearing and impiety. Then news came to Webster that there was a change in Colby. He decided to call on him to see if it was true.

Upon entering his sister's home, he noticed a large Bible opened on a table. Colby had been reading it before Webster's arrival. Colby immediately asked him, "Are you a Christian?" When he was assured of Webster's faith, Colby suggested that they kneel together and pray.

After the visit, Daniel Webster told a friend, "I would like to hear what enemies of religion say of Colby's conversion. Here was a man as unlikely to be a Christian as any I ever saw; he had gone his godless way until now, with old age and habits hard to change! Yet to see him a penitent, trusting, humble believer! That is nothing short of the grace of Almighty God."

The fruit of your faith is always found in your words and deeds. You cannot hide what you believe, for your words are your calling card. They will always give away the secrets of your heart.

Swearing

If you claim to be religious but don't control your tongue, you are just fooling yourself, and your religion is worthless.

James 1:26 NLT

He who guards his lips guards his life, but he who speaks rashly will come to ruin.

Proverbs 13:3

Let every man be swift to hear, slow to speak, slow to wrath.

James 1:19 KJV

There must be no filthiness and silly talk, or coarse jesting, which are not fitting, but rather giving of thanks.

Ephesians 5:4 NAS

Words Can Make a Difference

Two farmers lived next to each other, with nothing but a river dividing their properties. One day, the cows of one neighbor crossed the river into the other farmer's field of corn. They trampled and ruined about half an acre of the crop. The farmer who owned the damaged corn crop rounded up the cattle. He angrily cursed his neighbor and made him pay dearly for every ear of corn the cows had destroyed before he would return the cows to the other farmer.

Later that fall, the angry farmer awoke to find his hogs across the river. By the time he rounded up his wayward hogs, they had obliterated an entire potato patch. The angry farmer readied himself for a confrontation with the other farmer. But when he saw that his neighbor had no intention of hurling curses or exacting retribution, he was surprised. He said to him, "I cursed you for the damage your cows did, yet you said nothing about my hogs. Why is that?"

The neighbor replied, "Because I am a Christian."

Because of the words he did not say, the Christian farmer had the opportunity to witness to his neighbor. The angry farmer was converted that very night.

Temptation

God is never tempted to do wrong, and he never
tempts anyone else either.

James 1:13 NLT

For we do not have a High Priest who cannot
sympathize with our weaknesses, but was in all
points tempted as we are, yet without sin. Let us
therefore come boldly to the throne of grace, that
we may obtain mercy and find grace to help in
time of need.

Hebrews 4:15-16 NKJV

Use every piece of God's armor to resist the
enemy whenever he attacks, and when it is all
over, you will still be standing up.

Ephesians 6:13 TLB

Submit yourselves to God. Resist the Devil, and
he will run away from you.

James 4:7 TEV

The Flame of Faith

The son of a sea captain was confirmed one Sunday morning. Later that day in his cabin, the skipper was anxious to do what he could to reinforce the meaning of the service that his son had experienced that morning. He said to the young man, "Son, light this candle, go out on the deck, and return to the cabin with the candle burning."

"But, Father," the boy protested, "if I go on the deck, the wind will surely blow it out."

"Go," the captain said. "Do it."

So the son went. With much shielding and maneuvering, he managed to keep the flame burning. With a sense of relief and accomplishment, he returned to the cabin and showed the candle to his father.

His father then said to him, "Son, you were confirmed today. Your faith is still small. Yet you are growing up and are about to enter the big, tempting world that will do its best to snuff out the flame of your faith. You must keep it properly shielded." It was a vivid lesson the boy never forgot.

Temptation comes to everyone. It must be carefully avoided and consistently refused, so that the flame of faith will neither flicker nor die.

Temptation

If sinners entice you, turn your back on them!
Proverbs 1:10 NLT

No temptation has overtaken you but such as is
common to man; and God is faithful, who will not
allow you to be tempted beyond what you are
able, but with the temptation will provide the way
of escape also, that you may be able to endure it.
1 Corinthians 10:13 NAS

People are tempted when their own evil desire
leads them away and traps them.
James 1:14 NCV

The Lord knoweth how to deliver the godly out
of temptations.
2 Peter 2:9 KJV

A Needed Adjustment

A woman was working on her taxes one night when she made an unpleasant discovery. She noticed that her income from the previous year was higher than she had thought, so she owed more taxes than she had anticipated. Her son suggested she just "adjust" the figures. "I can't do that," she replied. "That would be lying."

Yet even as she spoke, the woman realized that she had already given in to the same temptation at work. At the bank where she worked, her boss had often asked her to change dates, add signatures, or "adjust" figures. That night she realized she could no longer participate in the deceit.

The next time her boss asked her to "help out," she refused. A few weeks later, the vice-president of the bank asked the woman if she had altered any documents. She admitted that she had and was then told that others in the organization had been put in the same position. She and several other employees met with the board of directors, the truth came out, and her boss was fired.

Nobody can rob you of your integrity. You alone have the power to diminish or destroy it by the way you handle temptation.

Tragedy

God is our refuge and strength, always ready to help in times of trouble.

Psalm 46:1 NLT

Though I walk in the midst of trouble, thou wilt revive me: thou shalt stretch forth thine hand against the wrath of mine enemies, and thy right hand shall save me.

Psalm 138:7 KJV

Even though I walk through the valley of the shadow of death, I fear no evil; for Thou art with me; Thy rod and Thy staff, they comfort me.

Psalm 23:4 NAS

Though he slay me, yet will I trust in him.

Job 13:15 KJV

From Suicide to Sunshine

There once was a man named Jeb. Early in his life, Jeb was so miserable that he attempted to kill himself by drinking poison. His suicide attempt failed, however. He succeeded only in burning his lips. As Jeb slowly recovered, he berated himself for his failure to kill himself. Yet as time passed, a different thought came to him: *Perhaps God has spared me for a purpose.*

From that moment on, Jeb decided it was his purpose in life to make others happy. Everywhere he went for the next thirty years, Jeb left a trail of smiles and sunshine. He was one of the happiest people you'd ever want to meet. He handed everyone he met a business card on which he had printed this message:

The Way to Happiness

Keep your heart free from hate, your mind free from worry.

Live simply; expect little; give much; fill your life with love; scatter sunshine.

Forget self.

Think of others, and do as you would be done by.

Try it for a week—you will be surprised.

Jeb's life could have ended in tragedy. Instead, God gave him a mission to help others find happiness. Have you included any happiness in your life?

Tragedy

Though you have made me see troubles, many
and bitter, you will restore my life again.
Psalm 71:20

This is my comfort in my affliction, for Your word
has given me life.
Psalm 119:50 NKJV

I cried out to the LORD in my great trouble, and
he answered me. I called to you from the world of
the dead, and LORD, you heard me!
Jonah 2:2 NLT

We know that in everything God works for the
good of those who love him.
Romans 8:28 NCV

From Tragedy to Triumph

One winter night, a man was driving two young women to a church meeting when they came upon a multiple-car collision. They were unable to stop on the slick road before they slammed into the back of a car. One of the girls, Donna, was thrown face-first through the windshield. The jagged edges of the broken windshield made horrible gashes in her face.

At the hospital, a plastic surgeon took great care in stitching Donna's face. Nevertheless, the driver dreaded visiting Donna. He expected to find her sad and depressed. Instead, he found her happy and bright, refusing to let the accident destroy her joy.

As Donna slowly recovered she became intrigued by the work of the doctors and nurses. She later studied and became a nurse, met a young doctor, married him, and then had two children. Years later she admitted that the accident was one of the best things that ever happened to her.

We are free to choose our attitude in every circumstance. We can choose to let trouble leave us depressed and weak, or we can choose to become happy and strong in spite of our trials. When we choose to have joy, our worst tragedies can be turned into our greatest triumphs.

Truth

Surely you heard of him and were taught in him in accordance with the truth that is in Jesus.

Ephesians 4:21

All Scripture is inspired by God and is useful for teaching the truth, rebuking error, correcting faults, and giving instruction for right living.

2 Timothy 3:16 TEV

The words of the LORD are flawless, like silver refined in a furnace of clay, purified seven times.

Psalm 12:6

The LORD hates . . . a proud look, a lying tongue, hands that shed innocent blood.

Proverbs 6:16-17 NKJV

Such a Good Feeling

Author Alice Walker once accidentally broke a fruit jar. Though there were several siblings around who could have done it, Alice's father turned to her and asked, "Did you break the jar, Alice?"

Alice said, "Looking into his large brown eyes, I knew that he wanted me to tell the truth. I also knew he might punish me if I did. But the truth inside of me wanted badly to be expressed. So I confessed."

Her father realized that the broken jar was an accident, so no punishment was administered. Yet what impressed Alice was the love she saw in her father's eyes when he knew that Alice had told the truth. "The love in his eyes rewarded and embraced me," Alice recalled. "Suddenly I felt an inner peace that I still recall with gratitude to this day whenever I am called upon to tell the truth."

A person always feels good after telling the truth, doing the noble thing, showing kindness, or meeting a need. We must remember, however, that we are to do what is right because it is right, not because it is effective in making us feel better or will bring us a reward—that, is the truth.

Truth

Do not testify falsely against your neighbor.
Exodus 20:16 NLT

We will lovingly follow the truth at all times—
speaking truly, dealing truly, living truly—and so
become more and more in every way like Christ.
Ephesians 4:15-16 TLB

[Jesus said]: "This is why I was born and came
into the world: to tell people the truth. And
everyone who belongs to the truth listens to me."
John 18:37 NCV

Now, O LORD GOD, Thou art God, and Thy
words are truth.
2 Samuel 7:28 NAS

The Sword of Flattery

In ancient Greece, Aristippus was a crafty philosopher with a hearty appetite for the "good life." Although Aristippus disagreed with the tyrant, Denys, who ruled over the region, Aristippus had learned how to get what he wanted in court by always flattering the king. Aristippus looked down his nose at the less prosperous philosophers who refused to curry favor in such a way.

One day, Aristippus saw his colleague Diogenes washing some vegetables. He said disdainfully, "If you would only learn to flatter King Denys you would not have to be washing lentils."

Diogenes looked up slowly and in the same tone of voice replied, "And if you had only learned to live on lentils, would not have to flatter King Denys."

Flattery is but the two-edged sword of lying and manipulation. A truthful compliment is always in order, but flattery that tells a person something that isn't true in hopes of gaining their favor is merely a hollow falsehood. What the flatterer doesn't realize, of course, is that with each false statement, he diminishes his own value. Eventually his words have no meaning even to the one who has been flattered. Choose instead to be a person of principle and always speak the truth, with love.

Wisdom

To be wise, you must have reverence for the LORD.

Job 28:28 TEV

If any of you needs wisdom, you should ask God for it. He is generous and enjoys giving to all people, so he will give you wisdom.

James 1:5 NCV

I [the Lord] will instruct you and teach you in the way you should go; I will counsel you and watch over you.

Psalm 32:8

Getting wisdom is the most important thing you can do. And with your wisdom, develop common sense and good judgment.

Proverbs 4:7 TLB

Jewels of Wisdom

Many years ago in South Africa a man sold his farm so that he might spend his days searching for diamonds. He was consumed with dreams of wealth. Yet when he had finally exhausted his resources and his health, he was no closer to his fortune than on the day he sold his farm.

One day, the man who had bought his farm spotted a strange stone in the creek bed. He liked its shape and placed it on his mantelpiece. A visitor noticed the stone and suggested that stone might actually be a diamond. The farmer quietly had the stone analyzed. Sure enough, it was one of the largest and finest diamonds ever found.

Still operating under great secrecy, the farmer searched his creek, gathering similar stones. They were all diamonds. In fact, the farm was covered with outcrops of them! The farm turned out to be one of the richest diamond deposits in the world.

The lessons of wisdom can often be learned in the relationships and experiences we encounter every day. Ask God to reveal to you what you need to know in order to live the life He desires for you. Very often the resources you need and desire are right in front of you.

Wisdom

"I guide you in the way of wisdom and lead you along straight paths. When you walk, your steps will not be hampered; when you run, you will not stumble," declares the LORD.

Proverbs 4:11-12

The LORD grants wisdom! His every word is a treasure of knowledge and understanding.

Proverbs 2:6 TLB

Your commands make me wiser than my enemies, because they are mine forever. I am wiser than all my teachers, because I think about your rules.

Psalm 119:98-99 NCV

What seems to be God's foolishness is wiser than human wisdom, and what seems to be God's weakness is stronger than human strength.

1 Corinthians 1:25 TEV

Wisdom

Three rough-looking fellows on motorcycles pulled up to a highway cafe. Inside, they found only a waitress, the cook, and one truck driver—a little guy, quietly eating his lunch.

The motorcyclists were angry because a truck had cut them off several miles back. They decided to take out their revenge on this innocent man. They grabbed his food, threw it across the room, and called him vulgar names. The truck driver quietly got up, paid for his food, and walked out.

Unhappy that they hadn't succeeded in provoking the little man into a fistfight, one motorcyclist said to the waitress, "He sure wasn't much of a man, was he?"

The waitress replied, "I guess not." Then, looking out the window, she added, "I guess he's not much of a truck driver either. He just ran over three motorcycles on his way out of the parking lot."

The majority of the problems we have in life are actually of our own making—either because of things we have said or done, or things we haven't said and haven't done. Now is a good time to ask God for the wisdom to make choices that will keep us out of trouble in the future.

Witness

Go, then, to all peoples everywhere and make them my disciples: baptize them in the name of the Father, the Son, and the Holy Spirit, and teach them to obey everything I have commanded you.

Matthew 28:19-20 TEV

When the Holy Spirit has come upon you, you will receive power to testify about me with great effect.

Acts 1:8 TLB

The followers went everywhere in the world and told the Good News to people, and the Lord helped them. The Lord proved that the Good News they told was true by giving them power to work miracles.

Mark 16:20 NCV

"You are my witnesses," declares the LORD, "that I am God."

Isaiah 43:12

What's Your Mission?

A businessman once saw a man carrying a backpack with a well-worn sign that read, "I will work for food." Although the businessman didn't usually respond to such pleas, this time he did. He invited the backpacker to lunch, and, in the course of their conversation, discovered that the man was not homeless, but on a mission.

The backpacker admitted that he had seen rough times early in his life, had made some wrong choices, and paid the consequences. But fourteen years earlier, while backpacking across the country, he had given his life to God. Ever since, he had felt God calling him to work to buy food and Bibles. Whenever he felt led, he would give the Bibles away.

His backpack was already filled with Bibles, but when the businessman asked him if he could use one more, the backpacker readily accepted. In return, he gave his benefactor his well-worn work gloves and asked, "Whenever you see these gloves, will you pray for me?"

The businessman replied, "You bet." The gloves sit on his desk today, reminding him to pray.

The Lord has a ministry designed to fit the unique qualities He has built into each one of us. Have you found, and accepted, your mission?

Witness

"You are My witnesses," says the LORD, "and My servant whom I have chosen, that you may know and believe Me, and understand that I am He. Before Me there was no God formed, nor shall there be after Me."

Isaiah 43:10 NKJV

He said to them, "Go into all the world and preach the gospel to every creature."

Mark 16:15 NKJV

Repentance for forgiveness of sins should be proclaimed in His name to all the nations, beginning from Jerusalem.

Luke 24:47 NAS

They that were scattered abroad went every where preaching the word.

Acts 8:4 KJV

Sing His Praise

Voltaire said that he would destroy, within just a few years, what it took Christ eighteen centuries to establish. He hoped to replace what he perceived as a faulty philosophy with a better one of his own creation. However, Voltaire's words were to become only hollow bragging. His own printing press was later used to print Bibles, and his log cabin became a storage place for them.

Reformation leader Martin Luther once said, "I pray you leave my name alone. Do not call yourselves Lutherans, but Christians." John Wesley expressed a similar sentiment when he said, "I wish the name Methodist might never be mentioned again, but lost in eternal oblivion." Charles Spurgeon said, "I look forward with pleasure to the day when there will not be a Baptist living. I say of the Baptist name, let it perish, but let Christ's own name last forever."

We err anytime we seek to sing our own praises. For the Christian, the only one truly worthy to be praised is the Lord God. Rather than exalt yourself today, seek to exalt the one whose name will last forever, and before whom every knee will one day bow. Let your witness for the Lord ring clear and true, unencumbered by any name but His.

Worry

Don't worry about anything; instead, pray about everything; tell God your needs and don't forget to thank him for his answers.

Philippians 4:6 TLB

Do not worry about tomorrow; it will have enough worries of its own. There is no need to add to the troubles each day brings.

Matthew 6:34 TEV

Give all your worries and cares to God, for he cares about what happens to you.

1 Peter 5:7 NLT

You will keep him in perfect peace, whose mind is stayed on You, because he trusts in You.

Isaiah 26:3 NKJV

Run to Win

In 1987, Eamon Coughlan ran a qualifying heat at the World Indoor Track Championships in Indianapolis. The Irishman was the reigning world record holder at 1500 meters and was favored to win the race handily. Unfortunately, with two-and-a-half laps left to run, he tripped and fell hard. Even so, Coughlan got up, and with great effort, managed to catch the race leaders. With only twenty yards to go, he was in third place, a good enough position to qualify for the final heat.

For some reason Coughlan looked over his shoulder to the inside. Seeing no one in his line of sight, Coughlan relaxed his effort slightly. What he hadn't noticed, however, was that a runner was charging hard on the outside. This runner passed Coughlan just a yard before the finish line, and eliminated Coughlan from the finals. Coughlan's great comeback effort ended up being worthless because he momentarily took his eyes off of the finish line and worried about would-be competitors instead.

One of the most important factors in your reaching your goals in life is to have single-minded focus. Don't let yourself become distracted by worry about what others do or say. Run your race to win!

Worry

The ones on whom seed was sown among the thorns; these are the ones who have heard the word, and the worries of the world, and the deceitfulness of riches, and the desires for other things enter in and choke the word, and it becomes unfruitful.

Mark 4:18-19 NAS

You cannot add any time to your life by worrying about it.

Matthew 6:27 NCV

Have I not commanded you? Be strong and courageous! Do not tremble or be dismayed, for the LORD your God is with you wherever you go.

Joshua 1:9 NAS

Peace I leave with you; my peace I give you. I do not give to you as the world gives. Do not let your hearts be troubled and do not be afraid.

John 14:27

A Box of Manure

A story is told of identical twins, one a hope-filled optimist who often said, "Everything is coming up roses!" The other twin was a sad and hopeless worrier who continually expected the worst to happen. The parents of the twins brought them to a psychologist in hopes that he might be able to bring some balance to their personalities.

The psychologist suggested that on the twins' next birthday, the parents put them in separate rooms to open their gifts. "Give the worrier the best toys you can afford," the psychologist said, "and give the hopeful child a box of manure." The parents did as he suggested.

When they peeked in on the worrier, they heard him loudly complaining, "I'll bet this toy will break. What will happen if I don't like to play this game? There's so many pieces, this toy won't last long; the pieces will all get lost."

Tiptoeing across the corridor, the parents saw their hopeful son gleefully throwing manure up in the air. He laughingly kept saying, "You can't fool me! Where there's this much manure, there has to be a pony!"

How are you looking at life today? As an accident waiting to happen, or a blessing about to be received?

Additional copies of this book and other titles
from Honor Books are available from
your local bookstore.

God's Little Lessons on Life
God's Little Lessons on Life for Dad
God's Little Lessons on Life for Mom
God's Little Book of Promises
God's Little Book of Promises for Mothers
God's Little Devotional Bible
God's Little Devotional Book Series
God's Little Instruction Book Series

If you have enjoyed this book, or if it has
impacted your life, we would like to hear from you.
Please contact us at:

Honor Books
Department E
P.O. Box 55388
Tulsa, Oklahoma 74137
Or by e-mail at info@honorbooks.com